FOOD ON THE GO

CHILLY'S

FOOD ON THE GO

EBURY
PRESS

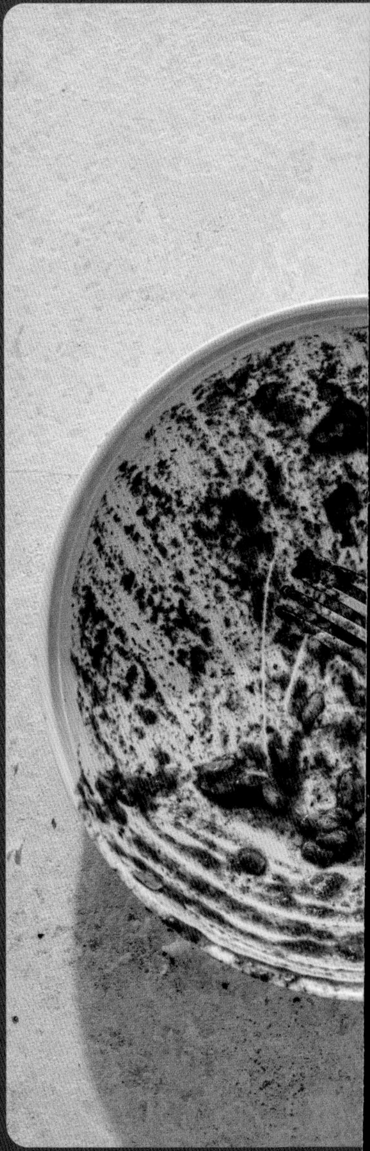

COOK

EAT

REUSE

CONTENTS

Welcome to Food on the Go.

At Chilly's we spend years designing and creating our products and we believe that the food and drink you put inside them deserves the same dedication to quality, functionality and satisfaction. So we decided to create our own cookbook full of simple and delicious recipes that work perfectly with your Chilly's products, bringing you inspiration and elevating your eating and drinking experience. Just like our other products, Food on the Go has been made to slot seamlessly into your lifestyle sharing our favourite recipes for brilliant breakfasts, satisfying lunches, delicious dinners, sustaining snacks and hot and cold drinks.

WELCOME

Since our founding back in 2010 by friends James Butterfield and Tim Bouscarle, our mission has remained the same: to accelerate the adoption and everyday use of reusable products. Chilly's has evolved into a pioneer of reusables and we want to keep growing this incredible community of like-minded people who are all committed to removing single-use plastics. We know that to do this we need to continue to design and make desirable and distinctive reusable products and together we'll create lasting habit change.

Est. 2010

· CHILLY'S ·

CHAPTER 1

BREAKFAST

Vg

Vegan porridge
with ginger & rhubarb

SERVES 2
PREP: 10 MINS
COOK: 15 MINS

450g/1lb young pink rhubarb, trimmed and cut into chunks
2.5cm/1in piece of fresh ginger, peeled and grated
grated zest and juice of 1 small orange
soft brown sugar or stevia, to taste
30g/1oz hazelnuts
125g/4½oz rolled or porridge oats
600ml/1 pint unsweetened oat or nut milk
a pinch of sea salt
4 tbsp dairy-free coconut yoghurt

TIP: ***Any nut milk is OK to use – try almond, hazelnut or macadamia nut.***

Oats are a healthy and delicious way to start the day. They are low GI and will make you feel full for longer, so you're less likely to snack during the morning. Just pop the porridge into your Chilly's Food Pot and breakfast or lunch is sorted.

1. Preheat the oven to 200°C, 400°F, gas mark 6.

2. Place the rhubarb in an ovenproof dish and sprinkle with the ginger and orange zest. Pour the orange juice over the top and cook in the oven for 15 minutes, or until the rhubarb is just tender but keeps its shape. Sweeten to taste with sugar or stevia.

3. At the same time, spread the hazelnuts out in a single layer on a baking tray and toast in the oven above the rhubarb for 10–15 minutes until golden brown and fragrant. Remove and wrap the nuts in a clean tea towel for 1 minute, then rub them vigorously in the tea towel to remove the skins. Set aside to cool, then chop coarsely.

4. Meanwhile, put the oats and milk in a saucepan. Add the salt and stir over a medium to high heat until it comes to the boil. Reduce the heat to a simmer and cook, stirring occasionally, for 5 minutes, or until the porridge thickens and is smooth and creamy.

5. Divide the porridge between 2 serving bowls or Chilly's Food Pots and top with the rhubarb, yoghurt and toasted hazelnuts.

OR TRY THIS ...

- Instead of an orange, use a juicy tangerine, satsuma, clementine or mandarin.
- Add a cinnamon stick to the rhubarb while it's cooking.
- Use almonds instead of hazelnuts.
- Use agave or maple syrup to sweeten the rhubarb. Non-vegans can substitute honey.

Breakfast muffins

A couple of these muffins are great for breakfast on the go when you're in a hurry. We love them and often make double the quantity and freeze one batch. Let them cool and when they are completely cold place them in labelled freezer bags. They freeze well for up to a month.

MAKES 12
PREP: 10 MINS
COOK: 30 MINS

2 tbsp olive oil
6 spring onions, thinly sliced
1 red or green pepper, deseeded and diced
1 bird's eye red chilli, diced
a handful of coriander, finely chopped
200g/7oz tinned sweetcorn, rinsed and drained
100g/3½oz lean cooked ham, diced
250g/9oz self-raising flour
1 tsp bicarbonate of soda
a good pinch of salt
2 medium free-range eggs, beaten
225g/8oz sour cream or Greek yoghurt
grated zest of 1 lime
100g/3½oz grated Cheddar or Monterey Jack cheese, plus extra for sprinkling

1. Preheat the oven to 200°C, 400°F, gas mark 6. Line a 12-hole muffin tin with paper cases.

2. Heat the oil in a frying pan set over a medium heat and cook the spring onions, red or green pepper and chilli for 5 minutes, or until softened. Stir in the coriander, sweetcorn and ham, and set aside.

3. Sift the flour, bicarbonate of soda and salt into a large mixing bowl and make a well in the centre.

4. Beat the eggs with the sour cream or yoghurt and lime zest, then stir into the flour with the cooled sweetcorn and ham mixture. Fold in the grated cheese.

5. Divide the mixture between the paper cases and sprinkle lightly with the extra grated cheese. Bake in the oven for 20–25 minutes until risen and golden brown. To test whether the muffins are cooked, insert a thin skewer into the centre – it should come out clean.

6. Leave the muffins to cool in the tin for 5 minutes before transferring them to a wire rack. They are best eaten warm or at room temperature on the day they are made. They keep well in a sealed container for 2 days.

OR TRY THIS ...

- Use a tinned jalapeno chilli or chipotle chilli flakes or powder.
- Use crumbled crispy bacon instead of ham.
- Instead of sprinkling cheese over the muffins before baking, use some sea salt crystals.
- Add a pinch of ground cumin.

Vg

PB smoothie bowl

You can whisk up a smoothie in less than 5 minutes, making it the perfect breakfast for busy people on the go. Smoothies are so versatile – just add your favourite fruit, vegetables, flavourings and nut butters (see the suggestions at the end of the recipe).

SERVES 2
PREP: 5 MINS

- 60g/2oz peanut butter
- 1 tbsp ground flaxseed or chia seeds
- 2 large bananas, sliced and frozen (see note)
- 120ml/4fl oz almond milk
- 200g/7oz non-dairy yoghurt, such as coconut or soya
- a few drops of vanilla extract
- 1–2 tsp maple or agave syrup (optional)

TOPPING

- 2 tbsp coconut flakes
- 2 tbsp chopped unsalted peanuts
- 2 tsp cacao nibs
- chia seeds
- peanut butter

1. Blitz the peanut butter, seeds, bananas, milk, yoghurt and vanilla extract in a blender until thick and smooth. Add maple or agave syrup to taste (if using).

2. Transfer to 2 bowls or Food Pots. Sprinkle with coconut flakes, peanuts, cacao nibs and chia seeds, and drizzle with peanut butter.

NOTE: ***Adding a frozen banana makes the smoothie bowl thicker and more creamy. Before freezing bananas, always peel them and cut into thick slices. Freeze overnight in a plastic bag.***

OR TRY THIS …

- Use almond butter instead of peanut butter and top with chopped or flaked almonds and a drizzle of almond butter.
- Add 1–2 tablespoons of cocoa powder.
- Top with sliced banana.

V

Quinoa breakfast bowl

Start the day right with some healthy quinoa, nutritious seeds, griddled vegetables and eggs. It's delicious, packed with protein and will keep you going right through to lunchtime. If you're in a hurry, no worries ... just microwave a pouch of ready-to-eat quinoa instead of cooking from scratch.

SERVES 2
PREP: 15 MINS
COOK: 25 MINS

- 75g/3oz quinoa (dry weight)
- 240ml/8fl oz vegetable stock
- ½ tsp cumin seeds
- ½ tsp fennel seeds
- 4 tbsp olive oil
- a handful of coriander, chopped
- 1 ripe avocado, peeled, stoned and diced
- juice of 1 lime
- 200g/7oz cherry or baby plum tomatoes
- 4 spring onions, trimmed and halved
- 400g/14oz tin black beans, rinsed and drained
- 2 medium free-range eggs
- sea salt flakes and freshly ground black pepper
- aji hot sauce, for drizzling

TIP: ***You can buy spicy aji (hot chilli pepper) sauce online and in specialist delis.***

1. Rinse the quinoa under running cold water, then drain. Heat the stock in a saucepan and when it starts to boil, add the quinoa. Reduce the heat, cover the pan and simmer gently for 15 minutes, or until the quinoa is tender and most of the liquid has been absorbed. When it's cooked, the 'sprout' or 'tail' will pop out of the seed. Turn off the heat and leave to steam in the pan for 6–8 minutes before draining off any excess liquid. Fluff it up with a fork.

2. Meanwhile, toast the seeds in a small dry frying pan set over a medium to high heat for 1–2 minutes, shaking occasionally, until aromatic. Remove from the pan.

3. Stir into the quinoa with 2 tablespoons of the oil, the coriander, avocado and lime juice. Season to taste with salt and pepper.

4. Heat 1 tablespoon of the oil in a griddle pan and cook the tomatoes and spring onions over a medium to high heat until just tender and starting to char. Add the beans and warm through quickly.

5. Fry the eggs in the remaining oil until the whites are set and are crisp and golden brown around the edges.

6. Divide the quinoa, griddled vegetables and beans between 2 serving plates or Food Pots. Top each with a fried egg and drizzle with aji hot sauce.

OR TRY THIS ...

- Substitute lemon juice for lime.
- Drizzle with West Indian or Mexican hot sauce instead of aji.
- Add some diced chorizo or crumbled crispy bacon.

V

Overnight chocolate & hazelnut oats

If you're not a morning person, this is the perfect breakfast for you. It takes only 10 minutes to prepare the night before – just pop the pots into the fridge and forget about them. When you get up the following day, top with fruit and nuts and you're good to go.

SERVES 2
PREP: 10 MINS
CHILL: 8 HOURS OR OVERNIGHT

- 100g/3½oz rolled or porridge oats
- 240ml/8fl oz unsweetened almond milk
- 200g/7oz yoghurt, such as Greek yoghurt or coconut milk yoghurt
- 2 tbsp chia seeds
- 2 tbsp chocolate hazelnut spread
- 2 tbsp chopped almonds or hazelnuts
- 1 small banana, sliced
- toasted hazelnuts or flaked almonds, to garnish

1. Put the oats, almond milk, yoghurt, chia seeds and chocolate hazelnut spread in a bowl and mix together well.

2. Divide the mixture between 2 glass screw-top jars or Food Pots and sprinkle the chopped nuts over the top. Cover with the lids or some cling film and chill in the fridge overnight, preferably for 8 hours, so the oats absorb all the liquid.

3. The following morning, remove from the fridge and top with the banana and the toasted nuts.

OR TRY THIS ...

- If you have a sweet tooth, add some stevia to taste to the oat mixture, or drizzle with maple syrup or honey.
- Use coconut milk instead of almond milk.
- Top with raspberries or strawberries.

OR TRY THIS …

- Top with blueberries, diced peaches or mango.
- Use soya, oat or coconut milk.
- Use peanut or cashew butter instead of almond butter.
- Sprinkle with chopped or toasted flaked almonds.

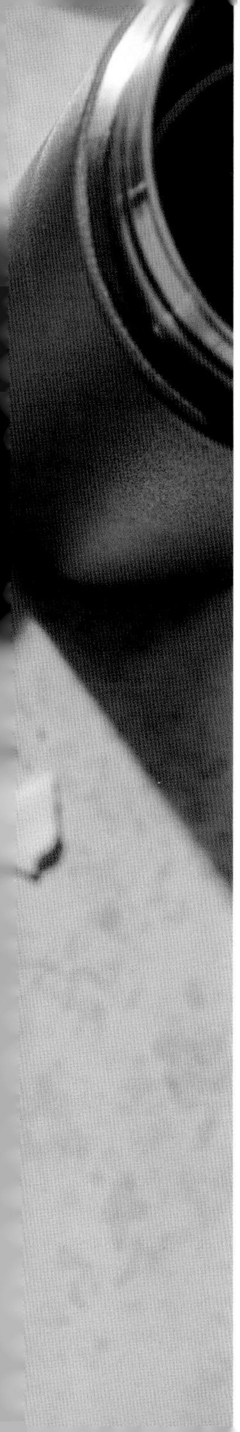

V

Chia seed chocolate powerpots

Chia seeds make a delicious 'porridge', which is so quick and simple to prepare. They have the amazing ability to absorb approximately 10 times their dry weight. They are a veritable powerhouse of nutrients and a rich source of protein.

SERVES 2
PREP: 10 MINS
CHILL: OVERNIGHT

1 large banana, mashed
1 tbsp almond butter
4 tbsp chocolate whey protein powder
300ml/½ pint unsweetened almond milk
a few drops of vanilla extract
6 tbsp chia seeds
60g/2oz raspberries
2 tbsp coconut flakes
2 tsp dark chocolate shavings
maple syrup, for drizzling

1. Put the mashed banana, almond butter, protein powder, almond milk and vanilla extract in a blender and blitz until smooth.

2. Transfer to a bowl and stir in the chia seeds, distributing them evenly throughout – the mixture should start thickening immediately. Pour into 2 Food Pots or screw-top glass jars and cover with the lids or some cling film. Leave to chill overnight in the fridge. The mixture will set by the following morning.

3. Just before serving, top with the raspberries, coconut flakes and chocolate shavings. Drizzle with maple syrup.

V

French toast sticks

with blueberry compôte

SERVES 2
PREP: 5 MINS
COOK: 20–25 MINS

- 2 medium free-range eggs
- 4 tbsp milk
- a few drops of vanilla extract
- a pinch of sea salt
- 3 thick slices white bread, cut into 2.5cm/1in wide strips
- light olive oil, for spraying
- 2 heaped tbsp cream cheese
- grated zest of 1 orange
- maple syrup, for drizzling (optional)

BLUEBERRY COMPÔTE

- 100g/3½oz blueberries
- 1–2 tbsp water
- 2 tbsp caster sugar
- a squeeze of lemon juice

For breakfast on the go, put the French toast sticks in one Food Pot to keep warm, and the blueberry compôte in another pot to stay cool. Dip the sticks into the compôte and enjoy with the cream cheese.

1. Make the blueberry compôte: put two-thirds of the blueberries in a small pan with the water and sugar. Place over a low to medium heat and cook gently for 10 minutes, stirring until all the sugar has dissolved and the blueberries burst. Add the remaining blueberries and cook for 5 minutes, until they soften but still retain their shape. Add a squeeze of lemon juice and set aside to cool a little.

2. Beat the eggs and milk together in a shallow bowl with the vanilla and sea salt until the yolks and whites are well combined.

3. Place the bread strips, a few at a time, in the eggy mixture and leave for 1 minute, or just long enough for the batter to penetrate the bread without it getting soggy and falling apart. Turn them halfway through to coat both sides.

4. Lightly spray a large non-stick frying pan with oil and set over a medium heat. When the pan is hot, carefully add a few soaked bread strips and cook for 2 minutes each side until crisp and golden brown. Remove from the pan and fry the remaining strips in the same way.

5. Serve the French toast sticks with the warm blueberry compôte and cream cheese, sprinkled with orange zest. If wished, drizzle the sticks with maple syrup.

OR TRY THIS ...

- Use pitted cherries instead of blueberries.
- Fry the French toast in a little melted unsalted butter instead of oil.
- Substitute thickly sliced brioche, or wholemeal or multi-seed bread for white.

Vg

Fruity acai bowl

This Brazilian-inspired dish is extremely healthy – acai berries are high in antioxidants and are a good source of fibre and protein. You can buy acai berry purée in packs in health food stores and some supermarkets.

SERVES 2
PREP: 10 MINS

- 2 x 100g/3½oz packs frozen acai berry purée
- 200g/7oz frozen mixed berries, such as blueberries, raspberries, strawberries, blackberries
- 1 large banana, sliced and frozen (see note on page 17)
- 2 tsp chia seeds
- 240ml/8fl oz oat milk
- 4 tbsp non-dairy yoghurt

TOPPING

- 2 tsp desiccated or shaved coconut
- 4 tsp porridge oats or granola
- 2 tsp hemp seeds
- a handful of fresh berries

1. Break the frozen acai purée into pieces by bashing it with a rolling pin.

2. Transfer to a blender* and add the frozen berries, banana, chia seeds, milk and yoghurt. Blend, starting on a low speed and gradually increasing it to high, until thick, creamy and smooth. As soon as it thickens, stop – do not overdo it.

3. Divide between 2 chilled bowls or Food Pots and top with the coconut, oats or granola, seeds and berries.

* ***You'll need a powerful blender to make this***

OR TRY THIS ...

- Add some dried dates or figs.
- You can use any milk: oat, almond, soya or dairy.
- Use fruit juice instead of milk.
- Add a handful of greens, such as spinach or kale, or some rolled oats.
- Top with chopped nuts, mixed seeds, cacao nibs or sliced banana.
- Sweeten, if wished, with maple or agave syrup, or honey.

Vg

Vegan breakfast bowl

Make this green quinoa tabbouleh the night before and you'll have a quick and easy breakfast the following morning. Or take it to work and enjoy as a packed lunch. If you like slow-dried tomatoes, make double the quantity and store in an airtight container in the fridge.

SERVES 2
PREP: 20 MINS
COOK: 1 HOUR

75g/3oz quinoa (dry weight)
240ml/8fl oz vegetable stock
175g/6oz curly kale or spinach, trimmed and chopped
a large handful of rocket
4 spring onions, sliced
a handful of mint, chopped
a handful of coriander, chopped
200g/7oz tinned chickpeas, rinsed and drained
1 ripe avocado, peeled, stoned and cubed
30g/1oz toasted almonds
seeds of ½ pomegranate

SLOW-DRIED TOMATOES

2 tbsp fruity green olive oil
a few drops of balsamic vinegar
1 sprig of rosemary, leaves picked
4 sprigs of thyme
8 baby plum tomatoes, cut in half
sea salt

LEMON DRESSING

2 garlic cloves, peeled
1 tsp white sesame seeds
¼ tsp sea salt crystals
1 tsp sumac
3 tbsp green fruity olive oil
juice of 1 lemon

1. Preheat the oven to 150°C, 300°F, gas mark 2.

2. Make the slow-dried tomatoes: mix together the olive oil, balsamic vinegar and herbs. Place the tomatoes on a baking tray, cut-side up, and pour the herby oil over the top. Season lightly with sea salt. Cook in the oven for at least 1 hour, checking them occasionally – don't let them brown or burn. When cooked, they should be quite soft and starting to shrivel and wrinkle, with a concentrated sweet flavour. Remove from the oven and set aside to cool.

3. Meanwhile, rinse the quinoa in a sieve under cold running water. Bring the stock to the boil in a large saucepan and add the quinoa. Reduce the heat, cover the pan and simmer for 12–15 minutes until just tender. Turn off the heat and leave to steam in the pan for 5 minutes. Drain well and fluff up the quinoa.

4. Make the dressing: using a pestle and mortar, crush the garlic, sesame seeds, salt and sumac. Gradually stir in the oil, then add the lemon juice.

5. Put the warm quinoa in a bowl and quickly stir in the greens, spring onions, herbs, chickpeas and avocado. Stir in the dressing and top with the slow-dried tomatoes. Sprinkle with the toasted almonds and pomegranate seeds.

OR TRY THIS ...

- Add some diced red chilli or crushed chilli or red pepper flakes.
- Drizzle with pomegranate molasses or hot sauce.
- Use baby spinach leaves for speed.
- Substitute toasted pine nuts for the almonds.

V

Refried beans breakfast burritos

SERVES 2
PREP: 10 MINS
COOK: 8 MINS

Burritos are perfect not only for breakfast, but for any time of the day. The smashed chipotle avocado is a delicious and super-speedy topping for toasted bread, bruschetta or griddled flatbreads.

olive oil, for brushing
4 spring onions, chopped
1 red chilli, diced
200g/7oz tinned refried beans
a handful of coriander, chopped
2 large wholewheat tortillas
a large handful of crisp lettuce, such as cos or iceberg, shredded
2 heaped tbsp hot tomato salsa
60g/2oz coarsely grated Cheddar cheese
sea salt and black pepper
Greek yoghurt or sour cream, to serve (optional)

SMASHED CHIPOTLE AVOCADO

1 ripe avocado, peeled and stoned
¼ red onion, diced
2 tinned chipotle peppers in adobo sauce, finely chopped
juice of ½ lime

1. Lightly brush a non-stick frying pan with oil and set over a low to medium heat. Cook the spring onions and chilli, stirring occasionally, for 3 minutes, or until softened. Stir in the refried beans and 2–3 tablespoons of cold water. Heat through gently for about 5 minutes, then add the coriander and season to taste.

2. Meanwhile, make the smashed chipotle avocado: mash the avocado coarsely in a bowl and stir in the onion, chipotle peppers and lime juice. Season to taste with sea salt.

3. Warm the tortillas in a low oven or on a lightly oiled griddle pan set over a low heat.

4. Spread the refried bean mixture over the warm tortillas and cover with the lettuce. Spoon over the smashed avocado and top with the tomato salsa and grated cheese.

5. Roll up the tortillas or fold in the ends to enclose the filling and then roll. Serve, if wished, with Greek yoghurt or sour cream.

TIP: ***If you don't have refried beans, just coarsely mash some drained tinned kidney beans or black beans.***

OR TRY THIS ...

- Use as a filling for warm pitta pockets or baked jacket potatoes.
- Substitute guacamole (see page 50) for the avocado.
- Add some griddled tofu, shredded chicken or roasted vegetables.
- Use chipotle pepper sauce instead of tinned peppers.

Breakfast frittata wedges

This recipe adds a spicy Spanish touch to an Italian-style omelette. Frittata is nutritious, easy to make and extremely versatile. It tastes good served at any temperature and is the perfect dish for any meal of the day.

SERVES 4
PREP: 15 MINS
COOK: 20–25 MINS

1 tbsp olive oil
1 red onion, chopped
2 garlic cloves, crushed
2 red peppers, deseeded and thinly sliced
225g/8oz spicy chorizo, diced
a good pinch of crushed chilli flakes
8 medium free-range eggs
a small handful of parsley, finely chopped
100g/3½oz grated Manchego cheese
sea salt and black pepper

1. Heat the oil in a large frying pan over a medium heat. Add the onion, garlic and peppers and cook, stirring occasionally, for 5 minutes, or until tender. Stir in the chorizo and cook for 2–3 minutes until it sizzles, releases its oil and starts to crisp up. Stir in the chilli flakes.

2. Meanwhile, beat the eggs and stir in the parsley and grated cheese. Season lightly with salt and pepper.

3. Pour the egg mixture into the pan, tilting it to spread it out evenly, and reduce the heat to low. Cook gently for 8–10 minutes until the frittata is set and golden brown underneath and only the top is runny.

4. Pop the pan under a preheated hot grill for 2–3 minutes until the top of the frittata is set, puffy and golden brown.

5. Slide the frittata out of the pan onto a plate or board and cut into wedges. Serve it hot, lukewarm or cold.

TIP: ***The frittata keeps well for 2 days if kept in a sealed container in the fridge.***

OR TRY THIS ...

- Use coriander instead of parsley.
- Substitute Cheddar for the Manchego.
- Omit the chorizo and add some fried potato chunks.
- Add a good pinch of smoked paprika to the beaten eggs.

V

Spicy corn fritters
with smashed avocado

SERVES 2
PREP: 15 MINS
COOK: 8 MINS

Serve these spicy fritters for breakfast, lunch or as a snack. Or try them using chipotle or habanero chillies and serving them with guacamole.

- 100g/3½oz tinned sweetcorn kernels, drained
- 75g/3oz self-raising flour
- 1 medium free-range egg, separated
- 1–2 tbsp milk
- 1 red bird's eye chilli, deseeded and diced
- 2 spring onions, finely chopped
- a small handful of coriander, finely chopped
- 2 tbsp groundnut oil
- salt and pepper
- chilli jam (available in some delis and supermarkets), to serve

SMASHED AVOCADO

- 1 large ripe avocado, peeled and stoned
- 1 red bird's eye chilli, deseeded and diced
- 1 garlic clove, crushed
- a few sprigs of coriander, chopped
- juice of ½ lime
- a few drops of olive oil

1. Make the smashed avocado: mix all the ingredients together in a bowl and mash with a fork until you have a chunky consistency. Cover and set aside while you make the fritters.

2. Put the sweetcorn in a small pan and cover with a little water. Bring to the boil and cook for 2 minutes. Drain well.

3. Sift the flour and salt and pepper into a bowl, then make a well in the centre. In a separate bowl, whisk the egg yolk and milk together, then beat it into the seasoned flour until you have a stiff batter.

4. Whisk the egg white until stiff in a clean, dry bowl. Using a metal spoon, fold gently into the batter in a figure-of-eight movement. Gently stir in the sweetcorn, chilli, spring onions and coriander, distributing them evenly.

5. Heat the oil in a non-stick frying pan over a high heat. When it's very hot, add small spoonfuls of the sweetcorn batter, flattening them out with a spatula. Cook in batches for 2 minutes each side, or until crisp and golden brown underneath. Remove with a slotted spoon and drain on kitchen paper.

6. Serve the fritters with the smashed avocado and some tomato chilli jam.

OR TRY THIS ...

- Fry the fritters in sunflower or olive oil.
- If you don't have tomato chilli jam, drizzle with Thai sweet chilli sauce.
- Use whole corn cobs and simmer in a pan of hot water for 7–8 minutes before stripping off the kernels and mixing with the other ingredients.

CHAPTER 2

SOUPS & HOTPOTS

Spiced sweet potato & coconut soup

SERVES 4
PREP: 20 MINS
COOK: 30–35 MINS

3 tbsp olive oil
1 onion, chopped
3 garlic cloves, crushed
2.5cm/1in piece of fresh ginger, peeled and diced
4 large carrots, chopped
3 celery sticks, diced
500g/1lb 2oz sweet potatoes, peeled and cut into chunks
600ml/1 pint hot vegetable stock
240ml/8fl oz coconut milk
2 tsp ground turmeric
½ tsp ground cumin
½ tsp grated nutmeg
a handful of parsley, finely chopped
6 extra-thin rashers smoked bacon or pancetta
salt and freshly ground black pepper

TIP: ***There's no need to add oil to the pan when you cook the bacon. Enough fat will run out of it to crisp it up.***

What's not to like about this colourful soup on a cold day? It's packed with healthy vegetables and anti-inflammatory spices and aromatics. Plus it keeps well for up to 5 days in a sealed container in the fridge.

1. Heat the olive oil in a large saucepan set over a low to medium heat. Cook the onion, garlic, ginger, carrots, celery and sweet potatoes for 10–15 minutes, stirring occasionally, until tender but not coloured.

2. Add the stock and bring to the boil. Reduce the heat immediately and simmer for 15 minutes, or until all the vegetables are tender.

3. Blitz the soup in batches in a blender or food processor until it is thick, velvety and smooth. Return to the pan.

4. Stir in the coconut milk and ground spices and reheat gently over a low heat. If the soup is too thick, just add some more coconut milk. Season to taste with salt and pepper and stir in the parsley.

5. Meanwhile, place a large frying pan over a medium to high heat and cook the bacon or pancetta, turning once, until golden brown and crisp. Remove and blot with kitchen paper.

6. Ladle the soup into 4 shallow bowls or Food Pots and crumble the crispy bacon over the top.

OR TRY THIS …

- Use pumpkin instead of sweet potatoes.
- Add a diced potato, butternut squash or some swede.
- Add some paprika (sweet or smoked).
- Fry a diced chilli with the onion and garlic or add some chilli powder with the spices.
- Top the soup with fried, thinly sliced mushrooms.

V Vg

Curried cauliflower soup

This golden soup is simple to make and freezes well, so why not make an extra batch and freeze it? You can use full-fat coconut milk but we prefer the reduced-fat version as the texture is less creamy. Use dairy-free coconut yoghurt if you're vegan.

SERVES 4
PREP: 15 MINS
COOK: 30–35 MINS

2 tbsp vegetable oil
1 large onion, chopped
3 garlic cloves, crushed
1 tbsp grated fresh ginger
1 fresh green chilli, diced
2 tsp ground turmeric
1 tsp garam masala
2 tsp black mustard seeds
2 tsp cumin seeds
1 large cauliflower, cut into chunks
1 large potato, diced
900ml/1½ pints hot vegetable stock
240ml/8fl oz reduced-fat coconut milk
salt and freshly ground black pepper
4 tbsp Greek or dairy-free yoghurt, for swirling
chopped coriander, to garnish

ROASTED CAULIFLOWER SLICES

1 small cauliflower, stem trimmed, cut into 1cm/½in slices
2 tbsp olive oil
2 garlic cloves, crushed
a pinch of dried crushed chilli flakes

1. Preheat the oven to 200°C, 400°F, gas mark 6. Lightly brush a large baking sheet with oil.

2. Make the roasted cauliflower slices: place the cauliflower slices on the baking sheet in a single layer. Combine the olive oil, garlic and chilli flakes, and drizzle over the cauliflower. Season with salt and pepper. Bake in the oven for 20 minutes, turning halfway, or until the cauliflower is crisp and golden brown around the edges and just tender (it should retain some 'bite').

3. Meanwhile, heat the vegetable oil in a large saucepan and cook the onion, garlic and ginger over a medium heat, stirring occasionally, for 6–8 minutes until softened. Stir in the chilli, ground spices and seeds, and cook for 2 minutes until they release their aroma.

4. Stir in the cauliflower chunks and potato, then add the hot stock. Bring to the boil, then reduce the heat and simmer gently for 15–20 minutes, or until the vegetables are cooked and tender. Stir in the coconut milk and season to taste with salt and pepper.

5. Blitz the soup, in batches, in a food processor or blender until smooth. Return to the pan and heat through gently without boiling.

6. Serve in bowls or Food Pots with a swirl of yoghurt and a sprinkle of coriander. Top with a roasted cauliflower slice.

OR TRY THIS ...

- Add some sweet potato or pumpkin.
- Swirl in some cucumber raita instead of yoghurt.
- Use ghee or coconut oil instead of vegetable oil.
- Garnish with toasted coconut flakes and nigella or black mustard seeds.
- Add some curry powder or garam masala with the ground spices.

V

French onion soup
with cheesy croûtes

This classic simple soup of meltingly sweet caramelised onions in a richly flavoured stock is very warming. You don't need a long shopping list for the ingredients, which most of us will have in the fridge or kitchen cupboards already.

SERVES 6
PREP: 15 MINS
COOK: 1½ HOURS

3 tbsp olive oil
1 tbsp butter
4 large onions, thinly sliced
2 tbsp plain flour
1.5 litres/2½ pints boiling beef stock
125ml/4fl oz dry white wine
1 bay leaf
salt and freshly ground black pepper

CHEESY CROÛTES

1 small baguette
2 tsp Dijon mustard
100g/3½oz grated Gruyère cheese

TIP: ***If you are serving the soup in Food Pots, just sprinkle the cheese over the toasted baguette slices and flash under the hot grill until it melts. Add to the Food Pots or serve separately with the hot soup.***

1. Heat the olive oil and butter in a saucepan over a low heat. Add the onions and cook very slowly and gently for 30–40 minutes, stirring frequently, until they are tender and golden and just starting to caramelise.

2. Stir in the flour and cook for 2–3 minutes, then add a little of the boiling stock, stirring until smooth and well combined.

3. Stir in the remaining stock and the white wine and bay leaf. Partially cover the pan and simmer gently for at least 40 minutes. Remove the bay leaf and season to taste with salt and pepper.

4. Preheat an overhead grill to high. Slice the baguette into diagonal rounds and lightly toast under the grill. Thinly spread some mustard over each slice.

5. Divide the soup between 6 bowls and float the toasted baguette slices, mustard-side up, on top. Sprinkle with the grated cheese and pop under the hot grill for just long enough to melt the cheese. Serve immediately.

OR TRY THIS …

- Use red onions instead of white ones.
- Add a few fresh thyme leaves with the wine and bay leaf.
- Gruyère is traditional but Emmental, with its nutty flavour, also works well.
- Imitate the French and add a spoonful of cognac.

Chicken choila

SERVES 2
PREP: 15 MINS
MARINATE: 15 MINS
COOK: 10–12 MINS

If you're a chilli afficionado, you'll love this dish of spicy barbecued or grilled meat, which is eaten widely throughout Nepal. The combo of fiery timur peppercorns, hot chillies and fresh and aromatic spices is not for the faint-hearted. Tempering them (roasting briefly) in smoking-hot oil gives the choila its distinctive flavour.

- 300g/10oz chicken breast fillets, cut into bite-sized chunks
- a pinch of crushed sea salt crystals
- 2 tbsp mustard oil
- 2 juicy tomatoes, skinned and quartered
- 2 spring onions, shredded
- ½ red onion, thinly sliced
- juice of ½ lime or 1 small lemon
- a small bunch of coriander, chopped
- a few crisp lettuce leaves, roughly torn
- 2 tsp fenugreek seeds
- 2 red or green hot chillies, shredded
- steamed rice or warm chapatis, to serve

CHOILA PASTE

- 1 tbsp ginger paste or grated fresh ginger
- 1 tsp garlic paste or 2 garlic cloves, crushed
- 1 tbsp tomato purée
- ½ tsp ground cumin
- 1 tsp chilli powder
- ½ tsp ground turmeric
- 1 tsp crushed timur or Sichuan peppercorns

1. Make the choila paste: mix all the ingredients together in a small bowl.

2. Stir the chicken with the sea salt and 1 tablespoon of the oil in a bowl until lightly coated. Set aside in a cool place or the fridge to marinate for 15 minutes.

3. Cook the chicken in a griddle pan set over a medium to high heat or over hot coals on a barbecue for 8–10 minutes, turning occasionally, until cooked through, golden brown and slightly charred.

4. Meanwhile, put the tomatoes, spring onions, red onion, lime or lemon juice, coriander and lettuce in a serving bowl. Mix together lightly, squashing the tomatoes to release their juices. Scatter the chicken pieces on top.

5. Heat the remaining oil in a frying pan set over a high heat. Add the fenugreek seeds to the smoking hot oil and cook for 1 minute, or until brown. Add the chillies and cook for 30 seconds. Stir in the choila paste and remove from the heat.

6. Quickly pour the hot spicy mixture over the chicken and salad and mix well until everything is lightly coated. Eat warm or cold with some steamed rice or warm chapatis.

OR TRY THIS ...

- Use crushed red chilli flakes instead of chilli powder.
- Substitute grilled duck breast meat or lamb fillet for the chicken.
- Serve with some spicy potato salad.
- If you don't have mustard oil, use sunflower or any vegetable oil.
- Add some mustard seeds with the fenugreek.

Chicken & shiitake miso soup

This healthy, cleansing soup is packed with nutrients and keeps well in a sealed container in the fridge for a couple of days. If you don't have fresh chicken, it's a great way to use up some cooked leftovers.

SERVES 4
PREP: 15 MINS
COOK: 25 MINS

- 2 tbsp olive oil
- 8 spring onions, sliced
- 2 garlic cloves, crushed
- 2.5cm/1in piece of fresh ginger, peeled and grated
- 450g/1lb skinned chicken breast fillets, thinly sliced
- 1 red chilli, deseeded and shredded
- 300g/10oz shiitake mushrooms, sliced
- 1 litre/33fl oz hot chicken stock
- 4 tbsp white miso paste
- 2 pak choi, quartered
- 400g/14oz pre-cooked rice or udon noodles
- a dash of lime juice
- 2 tbsp light soy sauce
- a handful of coriander, chopped
- lime wedges, for squeezing
- chilli paste or hot sauce, to serve

TIP: ***Use the best-quality stock you can buy for the best flavour.***

1. Heat the oil in a large saucepan set over a medium heat. Cook the spring onions, garlic, ginger and chicken, stirring occasionally, for 6–8 minutes, or until the vegetables are tender and the chicken is golden brown. Add the chilli and mushrooms and cook for 3–4 minutes.

2. Pour in the hot stock and bring to the boil. Reduce the heat to low and add the miso paste, stirring until it dissolves. Simmer gently for 10 minutes.

3. Add the pak choi and noodles and cook for 5 minutes. Stir in the lime juice and soy sauce.

4. Ladle into shallow bowls or Food Pots and sprinkle with the coriander. Serve with lime wedges and a bowl of chilli paste or hot sauce.

OR TRY THIS ...

- For a 'hot and sour' flavour add 1 teaspoon rice vinegar at the end.
- Add some beansprouts, mangetout or sugar snap peas.
- Instead of pak choi, add shredded spinach or spring greens.
- Serve sprinkled with white sesame seeds.
- Use white or chestnut mushrooms.

Easy beef ramen

This meal-in-a-bowl is comfort food at its very best. And the better the beef stock you use, the better the flavour. It's surprisingly quick to prepare and cook – perfect for an easy supper and with enough left over for tomorrow's packed lunch.

SERVES 4
PREP: 10 MINS
COOK: 15 MINS

- 250g/9oz ramen noodles (dry weight)
- 1 tbsp sesame oil
- 300g/10oz shiitake mushrooms, sliced
- 2 garlic cloves, thinly sliced
- 2.5cm/1in piece of fresh ginger, peeled and diced
- 1 red chilli, deseeded and shredded
- 1 litre/33fl oz hot beef stock
- 2 tbsp white miso paste
- 3 tbsp soy sauce
- 100g/3½oz mangetout, trimmed
- 4 spring onions, shredded
- 1 large carrot, shredded
- ¼ Chinese cabbage, shredded
- juice of 1 lime
- 400g/14oz lean rump or sirloin steak, all visible fat removed
- vegetable oil, for brushing
- chopped coriander, to garnish

1. Cook the noodles according to the instructions on the packet. Drain well.

2. Meanwhile, heat the oil in a large saucepan set over a medium heat. Cook the mushrooms, stirring occasionally, for 5 minutes. Stir in the garlic, ginger and chilli and cook for 1 minute.

3. Reduce the heat and add the stock, miso paste and soy sauce. Simmer for 5 minutes before adding the mangetout, spring onions, carrot and Chinese cabbage. Cook gently for 2–3 minutes until the mangetout is just tender but still crisp and the Chinese cabbage starts to wilt but still retains some bite. Stir in the lime juice.

4. Meanwhile, cook the steak in a lightly oiled griddle pan set over a high heat for 3–5 minutes until browned on both sides and cooked to your liking. Remove and slice thinly.

5. Divide the noodles between 4 shallow bowls or Food Pots and ladle the hot soup over them. Top with the steak, then sprinkle with coriander and serve.

TIP: ***You can also use brown miso paste, which has a more distinctive and earthy flavour than the white.***

OR TRY THIS ...

- Add some beansprouts or pak choi.
- Use chicken breast fillets instead of steak.
- Use egg noodles if you don't have ramen ones.

Chicken teriyaki meatballs

These tasty meatballs, served with rice and roasted broccoli, make a healthy supper. You can prepare the meatballs in advance and keep them in a sealed plastic container in the fridge until you're ready to bake them.

SERVES 2
PREP: 20 MINS
COOK: 20 MINS

350g/12oz minced chicken
45g/1½oz fresh white breadcrumbs
2 spring onions, diced
2 garlic cloves, crushed
1 tsp grated fresh ginger
1 small free-range egg, beaten
1 tbsp teriyaki or soy sauce
vegetable oil spray
115g/4oz basmati rice (dry weight)
1 tsp sesame seeds
sweet chilli or teriyaki sauce, for drizzling

CHILLI ROASTED BROCCOLI

1 small head of broccoli
2 tbsp vegetable oil
1 garlic clove, crushed
a few crushed chilli flakes
sea salt and black pepper

STICKY SAUCE (optional)

2 tsp cornflour
1 tbsp water
3 tbsp soy sauce
2 tsp mirin (rice vinegar)
1 tbsp clear honey
1 tbsp soft brown sugar
1 garlic clove, crushed
1 tsp grated fresh ginger

1. Preheat the oven to 200°C, 400°F, gas mark 6. Line a baking tray with baking parchment.

2. In a bowl, mix together the chicken, breadcrumbs, spring onions, garlic and ginger. Stir in the beaten egg and teriyaki or soy sauce to bind the mixture together.

3. With your hands, divide the mixture into 8 portions and roll each one into a ball. Space the balls out on the lined baking tray and spray lightly with oil. Bake in the oven for 15–20 minutes, or until cooked right through, crisp and golden brown.

4. Meanwhile, cut the broccoli through the central stem into thin slices. Place in a single layer in a roasting tin. Mix the oil with the garlic and chilli flakes, sea salt and black pepper, then drizzle over the broccoli. Add to the oven with the chicken and roast for 15 minutes until just tender and starting to char.

5. While the broccoli and meatballs are roasting, cook the rice according to the instructions on the packet.

6. Serve the meatballs, sprinkled with sesame seeds, with the rice and roasted broccoli, drizzled with sweet chilli or teriyaki sauce.

MAKE A SAUCE TO POUR OVER BEFORE SERVING:
Blend the cornflour and water in a small bowl. Put all the other ingredients in a small saucepan and stir gently over a low to medium heat until the sugar dissolves. Stir in the cornflour mixture and keep stirring until the sauce is thick and glossy.

OR TRY THIS …

- Sprinkle 2 tablespoons of grated Parmesan over the broccoli after 15 minutes and roast for a further 5 minutes.
- Add some diced chilli to the meatball mixture.

V Vg

Harira

SERVES 4
PREP: 20 MINS
COOK: 35–40 MINS
STAND: 5 MINS

3 tbsp olive oil
2 onions, finely chopped
3 garlic cloves, crushed
2 celery sticks, diced
2 tsp cumin seeds
½ tsp ground turmeric
a pinch of ground cinnamon
a pinch of crushed red chilli flakes
200g/7oz green lentils (dry weight)
2 large potatoes, peeled and cut into chunks
a handful of flat-leaf parsley, chopped
400g/14oz tinned chopped tomatoes
1 litre/33fl oz hot vegetable stock
400g/14oz tinned chickpeas, rinsed and drained
juice of 1 lemon
sea salt and black pepper
a handful of coriander, chopped, to garnish
harissa paste, to serve

This is our vegan version of a soup that is eaten after sunset during the month of Ramadan, when fasting ends until sunrise the following day. It is usually made with lamb, or sometimes chicken, but we have used lentils and chickpeas here and enlivened it with fiery harissa. Swirling this in at the end allows you to control the heat better, depending on your personal taste.

1. Heat the olive oil in a large saucepan set over a medium heat. Cook the onions, garlic and celery, stirring often, for 10 minutes, or until tender and golden. Stir in the cumin seeds, ground spices and chilli flakes and cook for 1 minute.

2. Add the lentils, potatoes and parsley and stir until they are glistening with oil. Add the tomatoes and stock and bring to the boil.

3. Reduce the heat and stir in the chickpeas. Simmer for 20–25 minutes, or until the lentils are cooked but not mushy and the potatoes are tender. Season to taste with salt and pepper and stir in the lemon juice. Remove from the heat and set aside for 5 minutes.

4. Ladle the soup into bowls or Food Pots and garnish with coriander. Swirl a little harissa paste into each one and serve.

OR TRY THIS ...

- Add shredded spinach or baby spinach leaves 5 minutes before the end of cooking time.
- Use chopped fresh tomatoes instead of tinned.
- Add a diced carrot with the onion and celery.
- Add some wholegrains, such as freekeh or farro, for a more filling meal.
- Swirl some yoghurt into the harira.

Chilled coconut corn soup

SERVES 4
PREP: 5 MINS
COOK: 15 MINS
CHILL: 2 HOURS +

This chilled soup is the perfect cooling lunch dish on a hot day. Vegetarians can omit the prawns and add some diced cherry tomatoes or baby spinach leaves.

1 tbsp Thai red curry paste
2.5cm/1in piece of fresh ginger, peeled and grated
420ml/14fl oz tinned reduced-fat coconut milk
300g/10oz tinned sweetcorn kernels, drained
420ml/14fl oz chicken or vegetable stock
12 raw peeled large prawns
juice of ½ lime
1 red bird's eye chilli, deseeded and shredded
a few sprigs of coriander, chopped
½ avocado, peeled, stoned and diced

TIP: ***Thai red curry pastes vary in their heat and intensity, so you may want to use 2 tablespoons if you like very spicy food.***

1. Put the Thai red curry paste in a large saucepan set over a low to medium heat. Stir gently until it releases its oil and starts sizzling. Add the ginger and cook for 30 seconds. Stir in the coconut milk, then add the sweetcorn kernels and cook gently for 5 minutes. Add the stock and simmer gently for 5 minutes.

2. Blitz the soup, in batches, in a blender or food processor until smooth, then return to the pan.

3. Set over a low heat and add the prawns. Cook for 2 minutes, or until they turn pink and are cooked through. Stir in the lime juice and check the seasoning.

4. Turn off the heat and leave the soup to cool in the pan. Transfer to a large container, cover with a lid and chill in the fridge for at least 2 hours.

5. Ladle the soup into 4 bowls or Food Pots and top each one with some chilli, coriander and avocado. Serve chilled.

OR TRY THIS ...

- Save some sweetcorn kernels and use as a garnish.
- Swirl in a little sour cream or yoghurt just before serving.
- For a creamier soup, use full-fat coconut milk or stir in a little crème fraîche or sour cream.

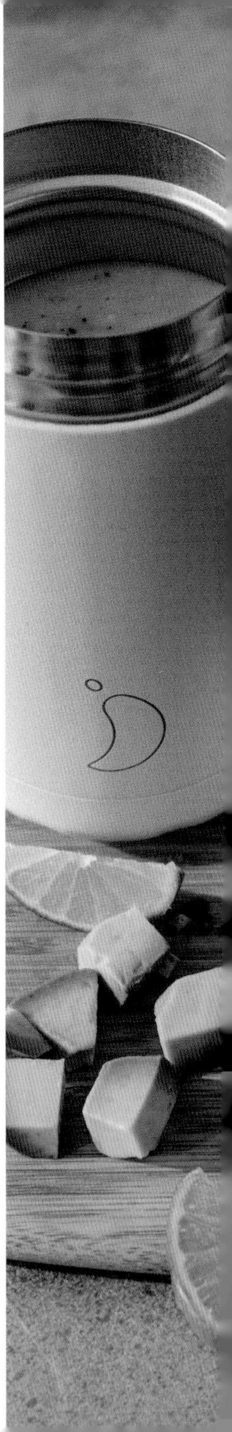

Chilli beef salsa pot

Stirring some freshly made tomato salsa into a pan of chilli spices it up and gives it a real kick. Depending on how much heat you like, you can vary the number and type of chillies you use. This chilli also makes a great topping for baked potatoes.

SERVES 2
PREP: 15 MINS
COOK: 40–45 MINS

1 tbsp olive oil
1 red onion, finely chopped
1 red pepper, deseeded and chopped
2 garlic cloves, crushed
225g/8oz extra-lean minced beef (max 5% fat)
2 tsp chilli powder
1 tsp ground cumin
1 tsp sweet paprika
400g/14oz tinned chopped tomatoes
240ml/8fl oz hot beef stock
400g/14oz tinned kidney beans, rinsed and drained
100g/3½oz tinned sweetcorn, drained
80g/3oz basmati rice (dry weight)
sea salt and black pepper
4 tbsp grated Monterey Jack or Cheddar cheese, to serve
2 tbsp sour cream or Greek yoghurt, to serve

TOMATO SALSA

4 ripe tomatoes, diced
¼ red onion, diced
1–2 hot chillies, such as jalapenos, diced
a large handful of coriander, chopped
juice of 1 lime
a good pinch of salt

1. Make the tomato salsa: mix everything together in a bowl. Check the seasoning, adding more lime juice or salt, if wished. Cover and set aside.

2. Heat the oil in a saucepan set over a low to medium heat. Cook the onion, red pepper and garlic, stirring occasionally, for 8–10 minutes until tender.

3. Stir in the minced beef and ground spices and cook, stirring occasionally, for 5 minutes until the beef is browned all over. Add the tomatoes and stock and bring to the boil.

4. Reduce the heat to low and add the kidney beans and sweetcorn. Simmer gently for 25–30 minutes, or until the beef is cooked, the vegetables are tender and the liquid has reduced and thickened. Stir in the tomato salsa and season to taste with salt and pepper.

5. Meanwhile, cook the rice according to the directions on the packet.

6. Divide the rice and chilli between 2 bowls, sprinkle with grated cheese and top with sour cream or yoghurt.

OR TRY THIS ...

- Use bottled or bought salsa from the chilled section in the supermarket instead of making it yourself.
- Serve with chunky guacamole (see page 50) or diced avocado.
- Instead of rice, use warmed flatbreads or tortillas.

Quick Thai curry

This curry is as simple and as good as it gets. It takes just a few minutes to make your own and the flavour is so superior. Double or quadruple the quantities given below and store the leftover paste in a screw-top jar in the fridge for up to 2 weeks or freeze it for up to 3 months.

SERVES 2
PREP: 10 MINS
COOK: 15 MINS

1 tbsp groundnut oil
400g/14oz chicken breast fillets, cut into strips
360ml/12fl oz coconut milk
6 Makrut lime leaves
100g/3½oz mangetout, trimmed
sea salt
a handful of Thai basil, shredded
steamed rice and lime wedges, to serve

THAI GREEN CURRY PASTE

2 lemongrass stalks, peeled and sliced
2 shallots, chopped
4–5 green chillies, diced
2.5cm/1in piece of fresh ginger, peeled and diced
2 garlic cloves, crushed
a small bunch of coriander, stalks, roots and leaves
2 tsp coriander seeds, crushed
1 tsp black peppercorns
grated zest and juice of 1 small lime
1 tbsp nam pla (Thai fish sauce)

1. Make the Thai green curry paste: put all the ingredients in a blender or food processor and blitz to a green paste.

2. Heat the oil in a large frying pan set over a medium heat and cook the chicken, turning occasionally, for 4–5 minutes until golden.

3. Add 2–3 tablespoons of the Thai green curry paste and cook, stirring occasionally, for 2–3 minutes. Add the coconut milk and lime leaves and simmer for 5 minutes. Add the mangetout and cook for 3–4 minutes until the sauce reduces and the mangetout is just tender but still quite firm.

4. Check the seasoning, adding salt to taste, and stir in the basil. Serve with steamed rice and lime wedges.

OR TRY THIS ...

- Serve with rice noodles instead of steamed rice.
- Use light soy sauce instead of nam pla.
- Substitute fine green beans for mangetout.
- Use reduced-fat coconut milk if you're on a low-fat diet.
- Use coconut oil instead of groundnut oil.

V

SERVES 4
PREP: 15 MINS
COOK: 20–25 MINS

Black bean chilli bowl

This Mexican-style smoky chilli takes very little time to make and keeps well in a covered container in the fridge for up to 3 days. This makes enough for 4 portions. For a vegan version, serve with coconut or soya yoghurt.

2 tbsp olive oil
2 red onions, thinly sliced
4 garlic cloves, crushed
1 tbsp ground cumin
1 tsp smoked paprika
2 tsp chilli powder
2 tbsp diced chipotles in adobo
800g/28oz tinned chopped tomatoes
1 tsp sugar
800g/28oz tinned black beans, rinsed and drained
juice of 1 lime
a handful of coriander, chopped
sea salt and black pepper
cooked brown rice or tortilla chips, to serve
sour cream or Greek yoghurt, to serve

GUACAMOLE

1 fresh green or red chilli, diced
½ red onion, diced
1 garlic clove, crushed
½ tsp sea salt crystals
juice of 1 lime
2 ripe avocados, peeled and coarsely mashed
1 ripe tomato, deseeded and diced
a small bunch of coriander, chopped
black pepper

1. Make the guacamole: blend the chilli, red onion, garlic and salt together using a pestle and mortar. In a bowl, stir the lime juice into the avocado. Add the tomato, crushed red onion mixture, coriander and black pepper, and mix everything together.

2. Heat the olive oil in a saucepan or a deep frying pan set over a low to medium heat and cook the onions and garlic, stirring occasionally, for 8–10 minutes, or until softened and golden. Stir in the ground spices, chilli powder and diced chipotles.

3. Add the tomatoes, sugar and black beans and cook gently for 10–15 minutes until thickened and reduced. Season to taste with salt and pepper and stir in the lime juice and most of the coriander.

4. Divide between 4 bowls and serve with brown rice or tortilla chips and guacamole. Sprinkle with the remaining coriander and add a spoonful of sour cream or yoghurt.

TIP: ***If you don't have any diced chipotles in adobo, use chipotle paste instead.***

OR TRY THIS ...

- For a really fiery guacamole, use Scotch bonnet chillies.
- Substitute kidney or pinto beans for the black beans.
- Use the chilli as a filling for burritos or wraps.
- Serve the chilli with quinoa or bulgur wheat.

CHAPTER 3

WRAPS & SANDWICHES

Spiced chicken & roast vegetable gyros

SERVES 2
PREP: 20 MINS
MARINATE: 30 MINS
COOK: 15–20 MINS

Gyros made with griddled meat or chicken and vegetables are classic Greek street food. They are wrapped in paper so you can eat them on the go. If you can't get hold of the thick, soft flatbreads that are traditionally used, just substitute large wraps or pitta breads. For extra flavour, add some tzatziki, tahini or hummus to the gyros.

SPICED CHICKEN

1 onion, quartered
3 garlic cloves, crushed
½ tsp ground cumin
½ tsp cayenne pepper
3 tbsp olive oil
300g/10oz chicken breast fillets, cubed
sea salt and black pepper

ROASTED VEGETABLES

1 small aubergine, thickly sliced
1 red pepper, deseeded and sliced
1 small red onion, cut into wedges
2 tbsp olive oil
1 tsp za'atar
1 tsp dried oregano

TO ASSEMBLE

2 large wraps or flatbreads
a handful of crisp lettuce, such as cos, shredded
2 ripe tomatoes, sliced
4 tbsp Greek yoghurt
hot sauce, such as sriracha, for drizzling
lemon wedges, to serve

1. Make the spiced chicken: blitz the onion, garlic, spices and oil in a blender or food processor. Transfer to a bowl and stir in the chicken. Season with a little salt and pepper, then cover and leave in a cool place to marinate for at least 30 minutes.

2. Brush the aubergine, red pepper and onion with olive oil on all sides. Sprinkle with the za'atar and oregano and season with salt and pepper.

3. Place a large, ridged griddle pan over a medium to high heat and cook the vegetables, in batches, for 2–3 minutes each side, or until just tender, slightly charred and golden brown. Drain on kitchen paper and keep warm.

4. Meanwhile, preheat the grill until it's very hot. Put the marinated chicken in a grill pan lined with foil and grill for 6 minutes, turning once or twice, until cooked right through and starting to char.

5. Warm the wraps or flatbreads in the griddle pan or in a low oven and place each one on a square of foil or baking parchment.

6. Divide the griddled vegetables and chicken between them and top with the lettuce and tomatoes. Drizzle with yoghurt and hot sauce. Fold the wraps around the filling and then roll up in the foil or parchment, folding in one end to stop the filling falling out. Serve with lemon wedges for squeezing.

OR TRY THIS ...

- Add some crumbled or cubed feta cheese.
- Sprinkle with chopped parsley, mint or coriander.
- Substitute lamb or pork fillet for the chicken.
- Cook the chicken on a griddle pan or hot barbecue.

Sushi sandwich

This Japanese-style sandwich takes a little while to make but you'll be pleased that you made the extra effort. We've used smoked salmon, but if you can get hold of it you could treat yourself and use raw sushi-grade salmon instead.

SERVES 2
PREP: 25 MINS
COOK: 15 MINS
CHILL: 30 MINS

115g/4oz sushi rice (dry weight)
2 tbsp rice vinegar
1 tsp mirin
2 large nori sheets
100g/3½oz thinly sliced smoked salmon
1 tsp wasabi paste
1 small avocado, peeled, stoned and thinly sliced
sesame seeds, for sprinkling
sea salt
soy sauce, to serve

PICKLED CUCUMBER

¼ cucumber
1 tbsp rice vinegar
1 tsp sugar
1 garlic clove, crushed

1. Cook the rice according to the instructions on the packet. Gently stir the rice vinegar and mirin into the warm rice.

2. Meanwhile, make the pickled cucumber: cut the cucumber vertically in half and, standing each half on one end, slice it really thinly from top to bottom. Alternatively, use a vegetable peeler or a mandolin to peel the cucumber into long ribbons.

3. Mix together the rice vinegar, sugar and garlic in a bowl, stirring well to dissolve the sugar. Add the cucumber strips and toss gently until coated all over. Cover and chill in the fridge for at least 15 minutes.

4. Place each nori sheet, shiny side down, on a square of cling film that is slightly larger than the nori. Take one-quarter of the warm rice and shape into a square on one of the nori sheets. Don't line it up with the sides of the sheet but position so that each side of the square is facing a corner of the sheet. Compact the rice with your hands, dipping them into cold water first, and press down firmly. Season with a little salt. Leave a border around the edges.

5. Place half of the smoked salmon on top and dot with wasabi paste. Top with half of the pickled cucumber and avocado slices and sprinkle with sesame seeds. Cover with a third of the remaining rice and press down firmly to level the top. Repeat with the other sheet and the remaining ingredients to make a second sandwich.

CONTINUED OVERLEAF

Sushi sandwich
CONTINUED

6. Now it's time to enclose the rice stacks. Pull one corner of the nori sheet over the rice into the centre of the stack and brush lightly with water. Fold the opposite corner of the nori into the centre and press down to attach it to the sheet underneath. Fold the remaining two opposite corners into the centre, 'glueing' them with water in the same way. You will have two sealed parcels with the nori enclosing the rice and salmon filling.

7. Wrap each parcel in the cling film and place in the fridge with a weight on top. Chill for at least 15 minutes. Cut each parcel in half with a sharp knife and serve with some soy sauce for sprinkling or dipping.

OR TRY THIS ...

- Use pickle red onions instead of cucumber, if you prefer instead of pickled cucumber.
- Vegetarians can substitute fried tofu for the salmon.
- Use prawns instead of salmon.
- Add some shredded Little Gem lettuce or spinach.
- Serve with pickled ginger.

Curried jackfruit wraps

For those of us eating less meat and dairy, here we've balanced a spicy jackfruit filling with a fresh mango chutney and soothing turmeric and ginger yoghurt for a delicious vegan lunch.

SERVES 2
PREP: 20 MINS
COOK: 25–30 MINS

- 1 tbsp sunflower oil
- 1 small red onion, finely chopped
- 2 garlic cloves, crushed
- 1 medium sweet potato, peeled and diced
- 300g/10oz tinned green jackfruit, drained and shredded with a fork
- 1–2 tsp curry paste
- 200g/7oz tinned kidney beans, rinsed and drained
- 120ml/4fl oz tinned coconut milk
- 100g/3½oz baby spinach leaves
- 2 large naan flatbreads
- 60g/2oz dairy-free coconut yoghurt
- ¼ tsp ground turmeric
- ½ tsp diced fresh ginger
- maple syrup, to taste
- shredded lettuce leaves
- ¼ small red onion, thinly sliced
- sea salt and black pepper

MANGO CHUTNEY

- 1 small ripe mango, peeled, stoned and diced
- ½ red onion, diced
- 1 hot red chilli, diced
- a handful of coriander, chopped
- a pinch of caster sugar
- juice of ½ lime

1. Make the mango chutney: put all the ingredients in a bowl and mix well, adding more sugar or lime juice if needed. Cover and set aside.

2. Heat the oil in a large frying pan set over a low to medium heat and cook the onion and garlic, stirring occasionally, for 6–8 minutes until tender but not browned. Stir in the sweet potato and jackfruit and cook for 5 minutes. Stir in the curry paste.

3. Add the beans and coconut milk and simmer gently for 10–15 minutes until the vegetables are cooked and the liquid has evaporated. Stir in the spinach and cook for 1 minute until it wilts, then season to taste with salt and pepper.

4. Wrap the naan flatbreads in foil and warm them in an oven preheated to 200°C, 400°F, gas mark 6 for 5 minutes.

5. Meanwhile, mix the yoghurt, turmeric and ginger in a bowl and sweeten to taste with agave or maple syrup.

6. Put a little lettuce on top of each naan and add the jackfruit filling. Top with the red onion, turmeric and ginger yoghurt and mango chutney. Fold the naan over the top and serve.

OR TRY THIS...

- Any beans are OK – try black beans or aduki beans.
- Use butternut squash instead of sweet potato.
- Substitute Greek yoghurt or cucumber raita for the turmeric and ginger yoghurt.
- Instead of naan, use warm pitta pockets or tortilla wraps.

Spinach and black bean quesadillas

SERVES 2
PREP: 10 MINS
COOK: 8–10 MINS

These quesadillas are so quick and easy to make and they taste great at any time of the day. Crisp and golden on the outside and oozing with melted cheese inside, they are the ultimate comfort food.

2 tbsp light olive oil
60g/2oz spinach leaves, washed, trimmed and shredded
75g/3oz tinned black beans, rinsed and drained
100g/3½oz grated Cheddar or Monterey Jack cheese
2 spring onions, thinly sliced
1 hot red chilli, diced
2 large flour tortillas
sea salt and black pepper
hot tomato salsa and sour cream, to serve

SMASHED AVOCADO

1 ripe avocado, peeled and stoned
1 garlic clove, crushed
a pinch of dried crushed chilli flakes
juice of ½ lime
a few drops of olive oil

1. Make the smashed avocado: put everything in a bowl and mash with a fork until well combined but still slightly lumpy. Set aside.

2. Heat 1 tablespoon of oil in a non-stick frying pan over a medium heat, add the spinach and cook, stirring, for 1–2 minutes – just long enough for it to wilt.

3. Transfer the spinach to a bowl and mix with the beans, grated cheese, spring onions and chilli. Stir well and season with salt and pepper.

4. Spread half of the mixture over half of one tortilla but not right up to the edge. Fold the other half of the tortilla over the top and press the edges firmly together to seal them. Repeat with the other tortilla and the remaining filling.

5. If there are still any pieces of spinach in the frying pan, remove them and add the remaining oil. Set the pan over a medium heat and when it's very hot, carefully add the tortillas. Cook for 3 minutes, or until they are golden and crisp underneath.

6. Use a spatula to flip them and cook the other side. When they're ready the filling should be heated through and the cheese melting.

7. Slide onto a board and cut into wedges. Sprinkle with sea salt and serve with the smashed avocado, salsa and sour cream.

OR TRY THIS …

- Use diced bottled jalapeno chillies or chipotle chilli in adobe sauce.
- Substitute refried beans or kidney beans for the black ones.
- Serve with hot sauce, pico de gallo (available in supermarkets), guacamole (see page 50), or smashed chipotle avocado (see page 28).

V

Sesame green falafels & mint yoghurt drizzle

MAKES APPROX. 24
PREP: 20 MINS
SOAK: OVERNIGHT
CHILL: 1–2 HOURS
COOK: 10–15 MINS

These falafels are a vivid, bright green in colour and taste delicious. The recipe makes 24 falafels – more than you need for a packed lunch – but they keep well when stored in an airtight container in the fridge. They also freeze well.

300g/10oz chickpeas (dry weight)
6 spring onions, sliced
a bunch of coriander, chopped
a bunch of flat-leaf parsley, chopped
a handful of mint, chopped
4 garlic cloves, crushed
1½ tbsp chickpea flour
1 tsp baking powder
1 tsp salt
1 tsp ground cumin
1 tsp ground coriander
a pinch of cayenne pepper
black pepper
white sesame seeds, for sprinkling
sunflower or vegetable oil, for frying
flatbreads or wraps and salad, to serve

MINT YOGHURT DRIZZLE

115g/4oz Greek or dairy-free yoghurt
1 tbsp tahini
1 garlic clove, crushed
grated zest and juice of ½ small lemon
a handful of mint, finely chopped

1. Put the chickpeas in a bowl and cover with twice as much cold water. Leave to soak overnight, then drain and pat dry with kitchen paper.

2. Blitz the chickpeas in a food processor with the spring onions, herbs and garlic. Add the chickpea flour, baking powder, salt and spices. Pulse until everything is well combined and the mixture holds together. If it's too dry, add 2–3 tablespoons of cold water. Add some black pepper and blitz again. Do not over-process – the texture should be coarse.

3. Take a spoonful of the mixture and, with damp hands, shape it into a small ball. Repeat with the remaining mixture. Roll them in the sesame seeds, then cover and chill in the fridge for 1–2 hours to help them firm up.

4. Meanwhile, make the mint yoghurt drizzle: put all the ingredients in a bowl and mix until smooth. Season to taste with salt and pepper. If it's too thick to drizzle, add a spoonful of water to thin it.

5. Pour the oil into a deep heavy-based saucepan to a depth of at least 7.5cm/3in. Place over a medium to high heat and when the temperature reaches 180°C/350°F (you can use a sugar thermometer to check), add the falafels, a few at a time. Fry for 4–5 minutes until crisp and golden brown all over, then remove with a slotted spoon and drain on kitchen paper.

6. Serve warm or cold in flatbreads or wraps with some salad and the minty yoghurt drizzle.

OR TRY THIS ...

- Add a diced green chilli to the falafel mixture.
- Serve with guacamole (see page 50) or sliced avocado.
- Drizzle the falafels with some hot sauce.

Lamb curry bao buns

SERVES 4
MARINATE: 30 MINS
PREP: 15 MINS
COOK: 1–1¼ HOURS

500g/1lb 2oz boned lean lamb fillet or leg steak, cubed
3 tbsp vegetable oil
2 onions, chopped
2.5cm/1in piece of fresh ginger, peeled and grated
4 garlic cloves, crushed
360ml/12fl oz hot water
3 cardamom pods
4 whole cloves
1 cinnamon stick
6 curry leaves
2 large ripe tomatoes, chopped
120ml/4fl oz coconut milk
bao buns or chapatis, to serve
a few sprigs of coriander, to garnish

SPICE RUB

1 heaped tsp curry powder
1 tsp chilli powder
1 tsp salt
½ tsp ground black peppercorns

You can now buy ready-made bao buns in some delis and supermarkets. The curry freezes well or can be refrigerated for a couple of days before reheating.

1. Make the spice rub: mix all the ingredients together in a bowl, then stir in the lamb until the cubes are lightly coated. Cover and leave in a cool place for 30 minutes.

2. Heat the oil in a large pan set over a medium heat and cook the onions, stirring occasionally, for 5 minutes until starting to soften. Add the lamb and cook for 5 minutes, turning the cubes occasionally, to brown them all over. Stir in the ginger and garlic and cook for 5 minutes.

3. Add the water, cardamom, cloves, cinnamon and curry leaves and bring to the boil. Reduce the heat and leave to simmer for 15 minutes. Add the chopped tomatoes and reduce the heat to low. Simmer gently for 30–40 minutes until the lamb is tender and the liquid has reduced.

4. Stir in the coconut milk and cook gently for a few more minutes until thick and creamy. Discard the whole cinnamon stick, curry leaves, cloves and cardamom pods.

5. Warm or steam the bao buns or heat the chapatis. Open the buns and fill them with the curry, or wrap the chapatis around the lamb filling. Garnish with coriander sprigs.

OR TRY THIS ...

- Use lean beef or skinned chicken thighs instead of lamb.
- Serve the curry with steamed rice or naan bread.
- Fresh mango chutney or a raita is a good accompaniment.

CHAPTER 4

SALADS

Cold chicken Milanese

with Sicilian fennel salad

The blood oranges and ruby-red pomegranate seeds in the salad make it look amazing. You can eat the chicken Milanese piping hot out of the pan or leave it to go cold and then slice it up the next day to eat with the salad as a packed lunch. The fennel stays crisp and the salad keeps well in a sealed container in the fridge overnight.

SERVES 2
PREP: 25 MINS
COOK: 6–8 MINS

2 large chicken breasts
plain flour, for dusting
1 medium free-range egg, beaten
45g dried breadcrumbs
25g grated Parmesan cheese
3 tbsp light olive oil
sea salt and black pepper

SICILIAN FENNEL SALAD

1 large fennel bulb, trimmed
2 juicy blood oranges
12 black olives, stoned
seeds of 1 small pomegranate
fruity green olive oil, for drizzling
sea salt crystals, for sprinkling

1. Make the salad: thinly slice the fennel and place in a bowl. Chop the small stalks and feathery fronds and set aside.

2. Cut the tops and bases off each orange and remove the outer peel and white pith with a sharp knife. Cut each orange horizontally into slices, then each slice into quarters. Place in the bowl with the fennel along with any leftover orange juice.

3. Add the olives, pomegranate seeds and reserved fennel stalks and fronds, and stir everything together. Drizzle with olive oil and some crushed sea salt crystals. Set aside.

4. Cut each chicken breast in half horizontally. Place between 2 sheets of

CONTINUED OVERLEAF

Cold chicken Milanese
CONTINUED

greaseproof paper or cling film and flatten with a mallet or a rolling pin until approximately 5mm (¼in) thick.

5. Put the flour and beaten egg into two shallow bowls, then lightly dust each chicken breast with flour on both sides and then dip quickly into the beaten egg. Mix the breadcrumbs and grated Parmesan in another bowl and dip in the chicken to coat both sides.

6. Heat the oil in a large frying pan set over a medium to high heat. When it's very hot, add the chicken breasts and fry for 3–4 minutes each side until cooked right through and golden brown and crisp. Remove and drain on kitchen paper. Serve hot or cold with the salad.

OR TRY THIS ...

- Substitute turkey or veal escalopes for the chicken.
- If blood oranges aren't in season, use any juicy oranges.
- Add some diced avocado to the salad.
- Serve the chicken Milanese hot with some spaghetti in tomato sauce.

Mykonos broccoli salad

SERVES 2
PREP: 15 MINS
SOAK: 5–10 MINS
COOK: 3–4 MINS

This healthy, crunchy salad is based on one that is served at Fokos, a seaside taverna in Mykonos. Broccoli florets are quickly blanched and tossed with raisins and nuts in a yoghurt dressing.

60g/2oz raisins
45g/1½oz coarsely chopped almonds
200g/7oz small broccoli florets
4 rashers streaky bacon or pancetta
¼ red onion, thinly sliced

YOGHURT DRESSING

120g/4oz Greek yoghurt
2 tbsp mayonnaise
1 tsp clear Greek thyme honey or maple syrup
a squeeze of lemon juice
sea salt and black pepper

1. Put the raisins in a bowl and pour some boiling water over them. Leave to soak for 5–10 minutes, or until they plump up. Drain and pat dry with kitchen paper.

2. Set a dry frying pan over a medium to high heat and, when it's hot, add the almonds. Toast them, shaking the pan frequently, for 1–2 minutes, or until golden brown and fragrant. Remove from the pan before they burn and set aside to cool.

3. Make the yoghurt dressing: put the yoghurt, mayonnaise and honey (or maple syrup) in a bowl with a dash of lemon juice and stir well. Season to taste with salt and pepper, and add more lemon juice, if wished.

4. Bring a large saucepan of water to the boil. Add the broccoli florets and blanch for 1 minute. Drain immediately and rinse under running cold water. Pat dry with kitchen paper and leave to cool.

5. Grill the bacon or pancetta slices until crisp and golden brown. Or fry them in a dry frying pan.

6. Put the broccoli in a large bowl with the red onion, raisins and most of the toasted almonds. Spoon the yoghurt dressing over the top and toss gently until everything is lightly coated. Sprinkle with the remaining almonds and crumble the bacon over the top.

OR TRY THIS ...

- Use toasted walnuts or pine nuts instead of almonds.
- Add some chopped sun-blush or sun-dried tomatoes.
- Stir a crushed garlic clove into the yoghurt dressing.
- Sprinkle with red chilli flakes.
- Substitute flaked almonds for chopped ones.

V

Spanakopita salad

This salad is actually a deconstructed spanakopita, composed of creamed feta, *horta* (cooked greens) and sesame filo triangles. It's very easy to make, and much healthier and lighter than the traditional spinach and feta pie.

SERVES 2
PREP: 20 MINS
COOK: 8 MINS

small sprigs of dill, to garnish
thin slivers of lemon zest, for sprinkling
a pinch of crushed red pepper or dried chilli flakes

FILO TRIANGLES

3 sheets filo pastry
45g/1½oz butter, melted
2 tbsp white sesame seeds

SPINACH HORTA

400g/14oz spinach, washed and trimmed (or a mix of spinach and wild greens)
2 tbsp olive oil
juice of ½ lemon
sea salt and black pepper

WHIPPED FETA

100g/3½oz feta cheese, crumbled
120g/4oz thick Greek yoghurt
grated zest and juice of ½ lemon

1. Preheat the oven to 200°C, 400°F, gas mark 6. Line a baking tray with baking parchment.

2. Make the filo triangles: place one sheet of filo pastry on a clean work surface and lightly brush both sides with melted butter. Lay another sheet on top and brush with melted butter, then cover with the last sheet and brush with the remaining butter. Cut into squares and then cut each square in half into triangles.

3. Sprinkle with sesame seeds and place the triangles on the lined baking tray. Bake in the oven for 8 minutes, or until crisp and golden brown. Leave to cool.

4. Meanwhile, make the spinach horta: steam the spinach or put the wet leaves in a large saucepan and cook, covered, over a medium to high heat, shaking the pan occasionally, for 2–3 minutes, or until the spinach wilts and is bright green. Drain well in a colander and squeeze out any excess water by pressing with a saucer. Transfer to a bowl and cool a little, then stir in the olive oil and lemon juice. Season to taste with salt and pepper.

5. Make the whipped feta: put the feta and yoghurt in a bowl and beat with a hand-held electric whisk until thick and creamy. Add the lemon zest and juice and beat well. Alternatively, use a food mixer.

6. Put some spoonfuls of the spinach horta on each serving plate or lunchbox and place some little heaps of the whipped feta on either side. Insert some filo triangles into the horta at regular intervals, so they stand up like sails on a boat. Sprinkle the whipped feta with dill, lemon zest and red pepper or chilli flakes.

OR TRY THIS ...

- You can make the horta with any greens: spring greens, kale, mustard greens, beetroot and turnip tops, sorrel, chard, wild rocket, purslane, dandelion leaves and amaranth.

V

SERVES 2
PREP: 25 MINS
COOK: 20–25 MINS

Bulgur bowl *with tomato fritters*

Crisp tomato fritters (*keftedes*) are a speciality of the Greek island of Santorini. We've served them with a healthy salad of crunchy, nutty bulgur wheat. This dish tastes delicious hot or cold.

- 100g/3½oz bulgur wheat (dry weight)
- 120ml/4fl oz vegetable stock
- ¼ red onion, diced
- 6 ripe baby plum tomatoes, halved
- ½ cucumber, diced
- 2 tbsp toasted pine nuts
- 2 tbsp pumpkin seeds
- a handful of mint, finely chopped
- juice of 1 lemon
- 2 tbsp fruity olive oil
- Greek yoghurt, to serve

TOMATO FRITTERS

- 200g/7oz ripe baby plum or cherry tomatoes, halved
- 2 spring onions, finely chopped
- 2 tbsp chopped mint
- 2 tbsp chopped dill
- 60g/2oz feta cheese, crumbled
- 60g/2oz plain flour
- ½ tsp baking powder
- 3 tbsp light olive oil, for frying
- sea salt and black pepper

TIP: ***For the best tomato fritters, use very juicy ripe tomatoes with lots of flavour and fragrance.***

1. Make the tomato fritters: put the tomatoes in a bowl and press down firmly with a spoon to crush them coarsely and release their juice. Stir in the spring onions, herbs and feta, and season with pepper. Stir in the flour and baking powder. If the mixture is too slack, add some more flour to bind it.

2. Take 1 tablespoon of the mixture and, with wet hands, mould it into a ball and then flatten it. Repeat with the remaining mixture and set aside. You should end up with approximately 8 fritters.

3. Put the bulgur wheat and stock in a saucepan set over a high heat and bring to the boil. Reduce the heat to low, cover the pan and simmer for 5 minutes. Turn off the heat and leave in the covered pan for another 5 minutes until the bulgur wheat is cooked and tender and has absorbed the liquid.

4. Transfer to a bowl and stir in the red onion, tomatoes, cucumber, pine nuts, seeds, mint, lemon juice and olive oil. Season to taste with salt and pepper.

5. Heat some oil in a large frying pan set over a medium to high heat. When it's really hot, add a few fritters (don't overcrowd the pan) and cook for 2–3 minutes until golden brown underneath, then flip them over and cook the other side. Remove with a slotted spoon and drain on kitchen paper. Keep warm while you cook the remaining fritters in the same way.

6. Divide the bulgur wheat between 2 serving bowls or lunchboxes and top with the fritters. Serve with Greek yoghurt.

OR TRY THIS ...

- Crumble some feta over the bulgur wheat salad.
- Serve with tzatziki or tahini sauce (see page 84).
- Substitute parsley or dill for the mint in the fritters and bulgur wheat.

Lemon & garlic chicken salad

SERVES 2
PREP: 20 MINS
COOK: 45 MINS

You can enjoy this aromatic dish hot or cold. It's so easy to make because everything cooks in a single pan while you assemble the salad.

300g/10oz small new potatoes, halved
250g/9oz chicken breast fillets, cubed
juice of 2 lemons
5 unpeeled garlic cloves
½ lemon, sliced
olive oil, for drizzling
a pinch of sweet paprika
sea salt and black pepper
harissa paste, to serve

SALAD

2 large ripe tomatoes, chopped
4 radishes, sliced
2 spring onions, thinly sliced
1 small cucumber, diced
1 small cos lettuce, thickly sliced
a handful of flat-leaf parsley, chopped
2 tbsp fruity olive oil
1 tsp pomegranate molasses
juice of ½ lemon
1 garlic clove, crushed
½ tsp sumac

1. Preheat the oven to 190°C, 375°F, gas mark 5.

2. Put the potatoes and chicken in a roasting tin and sprinkle with lemon juice. Tuck in the garlic cloves and lemon slices, then drizzle with olive oil and stir gently until the potatoes and chicken are lightly coated. Dust with paprika, season with salt and pepper and cover the tin with foil.

3. Bake in the oven for 30 minutes, then remove the foil and cook for a further 15 minutes until the chicken is cooked right through and golden brown. Slip the garlic out of the skins and squeeze them over the chicken.

4. While the chicken finishes cooking, make the salad: mix the tomatoes, radishes, spring onions, cucumber, lettuce and parsley in a bowl. Whisk the oil, pomegranate molasses, lemon juice, garlic and sumac until well combined. Pour over the salad and toss gently.

5. Serve the chicken and potatoes with the salad and some harissa on the side.

OR TRY THIS ...

- Use mint and coriander instead of parsley.
- Sprinkle the salad with pomegranate seeds.
- Substitute cubed sweet potatoes for the new potatoes.
- Add quartered red onions or sweet red peppers.
- Add some fried bread croûtons or diced pitta bread to the salad.

V Vg

SERVES 4
PREP: 15 MINS
COOK: 1¼ HOURS

- 5 tbsp olive oil
- 500g/1lb 2oz aubergines, cubed
- 1 large courgette, cubed
- 1 large onion, thinly sliced
- 4 garlic cloves, crushed
- 2 celery sticks, diced
- 1 red pepper, deseeded and cut into chunks
- a good pinch of crushed red chilli flakes
- 450g/1lb juicy tomatoes, skinned and chopped
- 85ml/3fl oz red wine vinegar
- 30g/1oz capers
- 60g/2oz stoned green olives
- 60g/2oz sultanas
- 1 tbsp sugar
- 45g/1½oz pine nuts
- a bunch of flat-leaf parsley, chopped
- sea salt and black pepper
- focaccia or toasted crusty bread, to serve

Caponata

This distinctive aubergine salad is like a Sicilian ratatouille. Eat it with grilled meat or fish, as a topping for crostini, or stir it into freshly cooked pasta. We've served ours with focaccia to mop up the sauce, but it also tastes good with couscous or bulgur wheat.

1. Heat the oil in a large deep frying pan or a sauté pan with a lid set over a medium heat. Add the aubergines and cook, stirring occasionally, for 5 minutes, or until tender and golden brown. Remove from the pan and drain on kitchen paper.

2. Add the courgette to the pan and cook, stirring occasionally, for 5 minutes, or until golden brown all over. Remove and drain on kitchen paper.

3. Add the onion, garlic, celery and red pepper and cook, stirring often, for 8–10 minutes, or until softened. Stir in the tomatoes and vinegar, then reduce the heat to low. Add the capers, olives, sultanas and sugar, then stir in the cooked aubergines and courgette. Season with salt and pepper.

4. Cover the pan and simmer on the lowest possible heat for 45 minutes, or until the vegetables are tender and the liquid has reduced to a thick sauce. Check the pan occasionally – if the caponata is too dry, add a little water.

5. Meanwhile, in a small dry frying pan set over a medium to high heat, toast the pine nuts for 1–2 minutes, tossing them gently, until aromatic and golden brown. Remove from the pan immediately.

6. Stir most of the parsley into the caponata and sprinkle the rest over the top with the toasted pine nuts. Serve lukewarm or cold with focaccia or toasted crusty bread.

NOTE: ***This recipe is for 4 servings. The caponata keeps well in the fridge for 2–3 days.***

OR TRY THIS …

- Stir in the juice of a squeezed lemon at the end.
- Substitute mint or basil for the parsley.
- Use tinned tomatoes or passata instead of fresh ones.

CHILLY

Sashimi salad lunchbox

If you like sushi, you'll love this. For best results, it's very important to buy really good-quality fresh salmon, preferably sashimi grade. However, if you're nervous about eating raw salmon but like Japanese umami flavours, you can substitute smoked salmon.

SERVES 2
PREP: 20 MINS
COOK: 10–15 MINS
STAND: 10–15 MINS

75g/3oz sushi rice (dry weight)
2 tbsp rice vinegar
1 tsp mirin
1 tsp black sesame seeds
1 tsp caster sugar
150g/5oz frozen edamame beans
1 carrot, thinly sliced with a vegetable peeler
½ daikon radish, peeled and cut into matchsticks
½ small cucumber, diced
1 ripe avocado, peeled, stoned and cubed
a large handful of frisée lettuce, shredded
150g/5oz sushi- or sashimi-grade salmon fillet, boned, skinned and cubed
toasted sesame seeds and nori strips, for sprinkling

WASABI DRESSING

2 tbsp light soy sauce
1 tbsp rice vinegar
juice of ½ orange
juice of ½ lime
1 tsp wasabi
a pinch of caster sugar

1. Cook the rice according to the instructions on the packet.

2. Meanwhile, heat the rice vinegar, mirin, sesame seeds and sugar in a small saucepan set over a low heat, stirring until the sugar dissolves. Mix gently into the rice, then cover the pan and set aside for 10–15 minutes, or until the rice is at room temperature.

3. Meanwhile, defrost the edamame beans according to the instructions on the packet.

4. Make the wasabi dressing: whisk all the ingredients together until well blended.

5. Put the edamame beans, carrot, daikon, cucumber, avocado and lettuce in a bowl and toss lightly in the dressing.

6. Divide the rice between 2 shallow serving bowls or lunchboxes. Pile the salad on top with the salmon cubes. Sprinkle with the toasted sesame seeds and nori strips.

OR TRY THIS ...

- Sprinkle with chopped coriander.
- Add some Japanese pickled ginger.
- Add some tomatoes, spring onions or red pepper.
- Instead of frisée, use cos or Little Gem lettuce.

Vg

Vegan poke lunchbox

SERVES 2
PREP: 15 MINS
MARINATE: 15 MINS
COOK: 15–20 MINS

This is a flexible feast and you can vary the ingredients according to what you have handy in your kitchen cupboards or fridge. It's delicious, satisfyingly crunchy and filling.

115g/4oz brown rice (dry weight)
1 tsp sesame oil
1 red chilli, deseeded and diced
2 handfuls of Chinese greens or pak choi, trimmed and roughly chopped
1 tbsp soy sauce
75g/3oz frozen edamame beans, defrosted
1 ripe avocado, peeled, stoned and cubed
2 spring onions, thinly sliced
2 tsp toasted sesame seeds
lime wedges, for squeezing
vegan hot sauce, such as sriracha, for drizzling (optional)

MARINATED TOFU

4 tbsp tamari or soy sauce
1 tbsp rice vinegar or lime juice
1 tsp sesame oil
1 tsp grated fresh garlic
1 tsp grated fresh ginger
250g/9oz extra-firm organic tofu, pressed (see page 99)

1. Cook the rice according to the instructions on the packet. Drain, leave to cool and then fluff up with a fork.

2. Make the marinated tofu: in a bowl, mix the tamari or soy sauce, vinegar or lime juice, oil, garlic and ginger. Cut the tofu into cubes and add to the bowl. Stir gently until coated all over. Leave to marinate for 15 minutes.

3. Heat the sesame oil in a frying pan set over a medium to high heat. Add the diced chilli and stir-fry for 1 minute. Add the greens and stir-fry for 2 minutes until they start to wilt. Stir in the soy sauce.

4. Divide the brown rice, stir-fried greens, edamame beans, avocado and marinated tofu between 2 bowls or lunchboxes. Sprinkle with the spring onions and sesame seeds. Serve with lime wedges for squeezing and hot sauce, if liked.

OR TRY THIS ...

- Use spinach or spring greens instead of Chinese.
- Substitute raw shredded red cabbage or kale for the greens and toss in a little tamari and sesame oil.
- Add beansprouts, cucumber, radishes, beetroot or pickled red onion.
- Drizzle with tahini or peanut butter sauce.

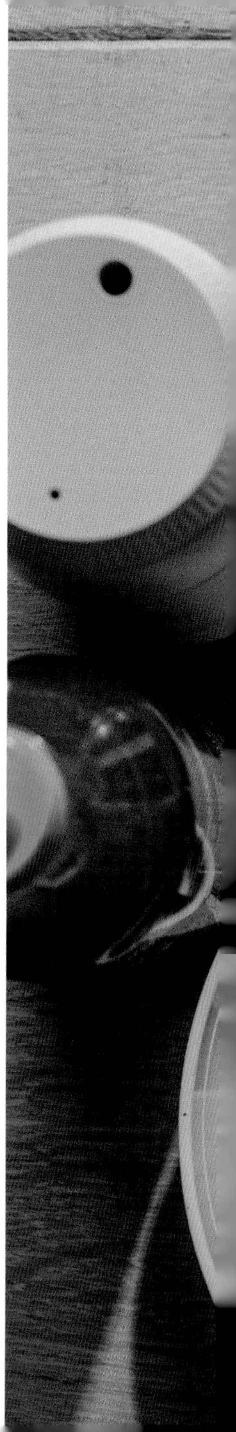

Kofta meatball salad
with flatbreads

These spiced Middle Eastern-style meatballs are so versatile and work well hot or cold. We've cooked ours in a griddle pan but they taste amazing grilled over hot coals on a barbecue on a warm summer's day. Make double the quantity and you'll have enough for packed lunches, snacks and picnics.

SERVES 2
PREP: 15 MINS
COOK: 5–6 MINS

- 350g/12oz minced lean beef or lamb
- ½ onion, grated
- 1 garlic clove, crushed
- a handful of flat-leaf parsley, chopped
- a handful of mint, chopped
- ½ tsp ground allspice
- ½ tsp ground cinnamon
- a pinch each of ground cumin, paprika and nutmeg
- ½ tsp salt
- oil, for brushing
- 2 large flatbreads
- crisp lettuce, sliced tomatoes and thinly sliced red onion, to serve

GARLIC TAHINI SAUCE

- 2 garlic cloves, peeled
- ¼ tsp sea salt crystals
- 3 tbsp tahini
- juice of ½ lemon
- 120g/4oz Greek yoghurt

1. Make the garlic tahini sauce: crush the garlic and salt using a pestle and mortar. Mix with the tahini and lemon juice in a bowl and stir in the yoghurt. Taste and adjust the seasoning, adding more lemon juice or a little water to thin it, if wished. Cover and chill in the fridge.

2. Make the koftas: mix the minced meat, onion, garlic, herbs, spices and salt in a bowl. Take small handfuls of the mixture and shape into 8 balls. Cover and chill in the fridge for 1 hour.

3. Lightly oil a griddle pan or frying pan and set over a medium to high heat. When it's hot, add the kofta meatballs and cook, turning occasionally, for 5–6 minutes until browned all over and cooked to your liking. Alternatively, thread them onto kebab skewers and cook over hot coals on a barbecue.

4. Warm the flatbreads and smear them with the garlic tahini sauce. Pile the lettuce, tomatoes and red onion on top and add the cooked meatballs. Fold over or roll up each flatbread in a square of foil and eat with your hands.

OR TRY THIS ...

- Serve with tzatziki, baba ganoush or hummus.
- Shape the kofta mixture into patties or long cylinders.
- Add some cayenne or chilli flakes to the kofta mixture.
- Drizzle some hot sauce over the koftas.
- Serve them in pittas or wraps instead of flatbreads.

Vg

Bang bang tofu salad

This vegan-friendly version of the classic bang bang salad uses protein-dense tofu instead of chicken. If you don't like peanuts, no problem – just substitute another nut butter such as cashew, almond or macadamia.

SERVES 2
PREP: 20 MINS
COOK: 5 MINS

- 100g/3½oz rice noodles (dry weight)
- 1 large carrot, cut into strips with a vegetable peeler
- 4 spring onions, shredded
- 75g/3oz beansprouts
- ½ cucumber, cut into thin strips
- a handful of coriander, chopped
- 200g/7oz extra-firm tofu, cut into 2.5cm/1in cubes
- 1 tbsp light soy sauce
- 1 tsp groundnut oil
- 60g/2oz chopped roasted peanuts
- 1 tbsp toasted sesame seeds

PEANUT BUTTER DRESSING

- 2 tbsp smooth peanut butter
- 1 tbsp groundnut oil
- 1 tbsp light soy sauce
- 1 tsp rice wine vinegar
- ½ tsp grated fresh ginger
- 1 garlic clove, crushed
- juice of 1 lime
- 2 tsp soft brown sugar
- a pinch of crushed chilli flakes

1. Make the peanut butter dressing: blitz all the ingredients together in a blender until smooth and creamy. If it's too thick, thin with a little water.

2. Prepare the rice noodles according to the instructions on the packet. Drain well.

3. Put the carrot, spring onions, beansprouts, cucumber and coriander in a bowl and mix gently together.

4. Place the tofu in another bowl with the soy sauce and stir gently. Heat the oil in a non-stick frying pan set over a medium to high heat, and cook the tofu for 4–5 minutes, turning occasionally, until golden brown all over and starting to crisp. Remove and drain on kitchen paper.

5. Add the rice noodles to the vegetables and toss gently in the peanut butter dressing. Divide between 2 shallow serving bowls or lunchboxes. Arrange the tofu on top and sprinkle with the peanuts and sesame seeds. Serve warm or at room temperature.

OR TRY THIS…

- Add some diced avocado.
- Vary the vegetables: try shredded Chinese cabbage or mangetout.
- Drizzle the salad with hot sauce.

Vg

Freekeh plant bowl

An ancient grain made from green durum wheat, freekeh is widely eaten throughout North Africa and the Levant. It is a good source of protein and is a good source of protein and dietary fibre.

SERVES 2
PREP: 20 MINS
COOK: 35 MINS

- 100g/3½oz freekeh (dry weight)
- 4 tbsp olive oil
- juice of 1 lemon
- a handful of flat-leaf parsley or coriander, chopped
- a handful of mint, chopped
- 2 spring onions, thinly sliced
- 6 medjool dates, stoned and chopped
- 400g/14oz tinned chickpeas, rinsed and drained
- 1 large carrot, cut into thin matchsticks or long strips with a vegetable peeler
- a handful of kale or spinach, washed and shredded
- 120g/4oz coconut yoghurt
- seeds of 1 small pomegranate
- sea salt and black pepper
- harissa paste, to serve

DUKKAH

- 1 tbsp almonds
- 1 tbsp shelled pistachios
- 1 tbsp white sesame seeds
- 1 tsp coriander seeds
- 1 tsp cumin seeds
- a pinch of sea salt crystals

1. Make the dukkah: set a non-stick frying pan over a medium heat, and when it's hot add the nuts. Toast, shaking the pan gently, for 1–2 minutes, or until golden and fragrant. Remove from the pan and add the seeds. Toast for 1–2 minutes, as above. Set aside to cool.

2. Using a pestle and mortar or food chopper, crush or pulse the toasted nuts and seeds until pulverised. They should retain a little texture and crunch. Mix in the salt and transfer to a sealed container.

3. Rinse the freekeh in a sieve under a running cold tap, then drain. Heat 1 tablespoon of the oil in a saucepan set over a medium heat. Add the freekeh and cook, stirring, for 2 minutes. Cover with cold water, increase the heat and bring to the boil. Reduce the heat and simmer for 25 minutes, or until al dente (tender but still retains some 'bite'). Drain, then rinse under cold water.

4. Transfer the freekeh to a bowl and stir in the remaining oil and lemon juice. Add the herbs, spring onions, dates and chickpeas, then gently stir in the carrot and kale or spinach. Season to taste with salt and pepper.

5. Divide between 2 bowls and top with the coconut yoghurt and pomegranate seeds. Sprinkle with dukkah and serve with harissa on the side.

OR TRY THIS ...

- Omit the chickpeas and serve with falafels.
- Add some chopped roast chicken and pour the chicken juices over the freekeh.
- Add some chopped preserved lemon, crushed garlic and broad beans.
- Use bulgur wheat or couscous instead of freekeh.
- Top with labneh instead of coconut yoghurt.

Vg

Low-carb teriyaki jackfruit 'rice' bowl

To keep this delicious salad low carb we've used cauliflower 'rice' and enhanced it with citrus, spicy, salty and sweet flavours. You can make it in advance and keep it overnight in the fridge until you're ready to cook the jackfruit.

SERVES 2
PREP: 20 MINS
COOK: 20 MINS

½ tsp sesame oil
1 tbsp dark soy sauce
1 tbsp mirin
1 tbsp rice wine vinegar
1 tbsp soft brown sugar
2 garlic cloves, crushed
1 tsp diced fresh ginger
400g/14oz tin green jackfruit in brine, drained
1 tbsp toasted white sesame seeds

CAULIFLOWER RICE

½ cauliflower, trimmed and cut into florets
1 tbsp groundnut oil
1 red chilli, diced
4 spring onions, thinly sliced
1 large carrot, peeled and grated
1 large courgette, grated
2 Makrut lime leaves, shredded
a handful of coriander, finely chopped

DRESSING

juice of 2 limes
2 tbsp nam pla (Thai fish sauce)
1 tbsp caster sugar

1. Make the cauliflower rice: pulse the cauliflower florets in a food processor until they have the consistency of rice-sized 'grains'.

2. Heat the groundnut oil in a wok or deep frying pan set over a medium to high heat. Stir-fry the chilli and spring onions for 2–3 minutes. Add the cauliflower and stir-fry for 4–5 minutes until just tender but still slightly crunchy. Transfer to a large bowl and mix with the grated carrot and courgette, lime leaves and coriander.

3. Make the dressing: whisk all the ingredients together, then sprinkle over the warm cauliflower and toss gently. Cover and chill in the fridge while you prepare the jackfruit.

4. Mix the sesame oil, soy sauce, mirin, vinegar, sugar, garlic and ginger in a bowl. Dry the jackfruit pieces with kitchen paper and shred with 2 forks.

5. Heat a non-stick frying pan over a medium to high heat (with no oil or water) and add the jackfruit. Cook for 4–5 minutes, stirring and tossing, until dry and starting to colour. Stir in the sesame and soy mixture and cook gently until it reduces and the jackfruit is well glazed and glossy.

6. Divide the cauli rice between 2 bowls, lunchboxes or Food Pots and add the teriyaki-glazed jackfruit. Sprinkle with sesame seeds and serve.

TIP: ***Vegans can substitute vegan soy sauce or vegan fish sauce for the nam pla in the dressing.***

OR TRY THIS ...

- Use black sesame seeds instead of white.
- You can use the jackfruit chunks whole instead of shredding them.
- Serve with wilted spinach or spring greens.

Jewelled couscous
with shrimp

SERVES 2
PREP: 20 mins
SOAK: 15 mins
COOK: 5 mins

85g/3oz couscous (dry weight)
180ml/6fl oz boiling vegetable stock
2 tbsp olive oil
30g/1oz sultanas
30g/1oz pine nuts
300g/10oz raw peeled large prawns
2 tbsp pumpkin seeds
a handful of flat-leaf parsley, chopped
a bunch of mint, chopped
juice of 1 lemon
seeds of ½ pomegranate
sea salt and black pepper
harissa paste and labneh (available in some delis and supermarkets), to serve

SPICY PASTE

1 tsp coriander seeds
1 tsp cumin seeds
2 garlic cloves, skinned
1 small red chilli, diced
2–3 tbsp Greek yoghurt

TIP: ***You can make the spice paste in advance and leave the prawns to marinate for a few hours in the fridge.***

Couscous is so quick and easy to prepare and is great at absorbing flavours. This dish tastes good served warm for supper or cold as a lunchbox salad the following day.

1. Put the couscous in a large heatproof bowl and pour over the boiling vegetable stock. Stir in the olive oil, cover the bowl and set aside for 12–15 minutes until the grains swell and absorb the liquid.

2. Put the sultanas in a bowl and pour some boiling water over them. Leave to soak for 5–10 minutes until plump and softened. Drain well.

3. Meanwhile, set a dry frying pan over a medium heat and when it's hot, add the pine nuts. Toast lightly by tossing them for 1–2 minutes until they are golden brown and fragrant. Remove from the pan.

4. Make the spicy paste: grind the coriander and cumin seeds using a pestle and mortar. Add the garlic and chilli and keep grinding and crushing until you have a thick paste. Transfer to a bowl and stir in the yoghurt. Add the prawns and coat them lightly with the mixture.

5. Gently mix the pine nuts, sultanas, pumpkin seeds and most of the herbs into the couscous. Stir in the lemon juice and pomegranate seeds and season to taste with salt and pepper.

6. Heat a non-stick griddle pan over a medium heat, and when it's very hot, add the prawns. Cook quickly for 1–2 minutes each side until they turn pink and are cooked through.

7. Divide the couscous between 2 bowls and pile the griddled prawns on top. Sprinkle with the remaining herbs and serve with a dash of fiery harissa and a spoonful of labneh.

OR TRY THIS ...

- Instead of prawns, top with griddled chicken, halloumi or tofu.
- Use lime juice instead of lemon and add avocado.
- Add some chopped preserved lemon to the couscous.

Griddled chicken

with curried potato & mango salads

SERVES 2
PREP: 20 MINS
COOK: 25–30 MINS

¼ red onion, chopped
2 garlic cloves, crushed
a pinch of chilli powder
1 tbsp cider vinegar
1 tbsp olive oil, plus extra for brushing
juice of ½ orange
4 chicken thigh fillets, flattened
sea salt and black pepper

CURRIED POTATO SALAD

400g/14oz new potatoes
1 tbsp Thai green curry paste
4 tbsp mayonnaise
4 spring onions, sliced
a small handful of coriander, chopped

MANGO SALAD

1 small ripe mango, cut into matchsticks
½ red pepper, deseeded and thinly sliced
1 red chilli, deseeded and shredded
a few lettuce leaves, torn
a few sprigs of coriander
1 tsp soy sauce or tamari
1 tsp vegetable or toasted sesame oil
juice of ½ lime
½ tsp caster sugar

This griddled chicken tastes delicious with either or both of these salads, and is tasty hot or cold.

1. Cook the potatoes in a large saucepan of salted boiling water for 15 minutes, or until they are just tender but not mushy. Drain and let them cool a little.

2. When the potatoes are cool enough to handle, cut them into thick slices or chunks and place in a bowl.

3. Mix the curry paste with the mayonnaise, spring onions and coriander. If it's too thick, add some more mayonnaise. Season to taste, and if it's not hot and spicy enough for your liking, add some more curry paste. Gently stir into the warm potatoes until they are coated.

4. In a food chopper or blender, blitz the red onion, garlic, chilli powder, vinegar, olive oil and orange juice. Place the chicken in a bowl and coat in the spicy marinade.

5. Lightly brush a ridged griddle pan with oil and set over a medium to high heat. When it's hot, add the chicken and cook for 5–6 minutes each side, or until attractively striped, golden brown and cooked right through.

6. While the chicken is cooking, make the mango salad: put the mango, red pepper, chilli and lettuce in a bowl with the coriander. Mix the soy sauce or tamari, oil, lime juice and sugar and use to gently toss the salad.

7. Serve the chicken hot or cold with the curried potato and mango salads.

OR TRY THIS ...

- Use chicken breast fillets instead of thighs.
- Use Thai red curry paste instead of green.
- Substitute a papaya for the mango.

Prawn anticuchos

SERVES 2
PREP: 15 MINS
MARINATE: 1 HOUR
COOK: 15–20 MINS

2 tbsp white wine vinegar
1 tbsp olive oil, plus extra for brushing
1 tbsp aji panca
juice of 1 lime
2 garlic cloves, crushed
½ tsp freshly ground black peppercorns
½ tsp ground cumin
¼ tsp ground turmeric
a good pinch of salt
8 large raw peeled large prawns
300ml/½ pint vegetable stock
115g/4oz quinoa (dry weight)
lime wedges, for squeezing

DIPPING SAUCE

2 red chillies, deseeded and shredded
2.5cm/1in piece of fresh ginger, peeled and diced
a handful of coriander, chopped
2 tbsp nam pla (Thai fish sauce)
2 tsp sugar
juice of 1–2 limes

Anticuchos **(spicy meat, chicken or fish kebabs) are a popular dish and street food in Peru. They are traditionally cooked over hot coals or wood on a barbecue but we've used a griddle pan. You can buy *aji panca*, a smoky, Peruvian red chilli pepper which is sun-dried and then ground, online or in specialist stores.**

1. Mix together the vinegar, oil, aji panca, lime juice, garlic, spices and salt in a bowl. Add the prawns and stir gently until well coated. Cover and leave in the fridge for 1 hour to marinate.

2. Meanwhile, make the dipping sauce: mix all the ingredients together in a bowl, stirring to dissolve the sugar.

3. Heat the stock in a saucepan set over a high heat and when it starts to boil, add the quinoa. Reduce the heat, cover and simmer gently for 15 minutes, or until tender and most of the broth has been absorbed. Turn off the heat and leave to steam in the pan for 5–8 minutes. Drain off the excess liquid and fluff up the quinoa with a fork. Set aside to cool a little.

4. Thread the prawns in their spicy marinade onto 2 wooden skewers (see note below). Brush a griddle pan with oil and set over a high heat. When it's hot, add the prawn skewers and cook for 1–2 minutes each side until the prawns turn pink.

5. Serve the prawns on a bed of quinoa with the dipping sauce and lime wedges for squeezing.

NOTE: ***When using wooden skewers, soak them overnight in cold water before threading to prevent them burning.***

OR TRY THIS ...

- Use steak, chicken or squid instead of prawns.
- Serve with green chimichurri sauce.
- Instead of quinoa, serve with earthy brown rice.

Thai-style chicken & rice salad

An aromatic salad which is simplicity to make and tastes even better if kept in the fridge overnight and eaten the following day. If you like Thai food and flavours you'll love this.

SERVES 2
PREP: 15 MINS
COOK: 15 MINS

- 150g/5oz Thai jasmine rice (dry weight)
- 2 tbsp groundnut oil
- 1 lemongrass stalk, peeled and thinly sliced
- 2 red bird's eye chillies, deseeded and shredded
- 1cm/½in piece of fresh ginger, peeled and diced
- 6 spring onions, thinly sliced
- 2 garlic cloves, crushed
- a large handful of coriander, chopped
- a handful of Thai basil, chopped
- 200g/7oz cooked chicken breast fillets, diced
- sea salt and black pepper
- chopped peanuts or cashews, for sprinkling

DRESSING

- 2 tbsp nam pla (Thai fish sauce)
- juice of 1 lime
- 1 tbsp olive or sesame oil
- 1 tbsp caster sugar

1. Cook the rice according to the instructions on the packet. Leave the rice in the pan, covered, for 10 minutes.

2. Meanwhile, make the dressing: mix all the ingredients together in a bowl.

3. Heat the oil in a wok or frying pan set over a medium to high heat. Add the lemongrass, chillies, ginger, spring onions and garlic and stir-fry, without browning, for 2 minutes. Remove from the pan.

4. Fluff up the cooked rice with a fork and transfer to a bowl. Gently stir in the stir-fried chilli mixture and most of the herbs. Mix in the chicken and the dressing, then check the seasoning, adding salt and pepper to taste.

5. Cover and chill in the fridge before serving in 2 bowls or lunchboxes, sprinkled with the remaining herbs and the chopped nuts.

TIP: ***For a vegetarian version, use stir-fried tofu instead of chicken.***

OR TRY THIS ...

- Add some thinly sliced Makrut lime leaves.
- Vary the herbs: try mint or chives.
- Add some sprouted seeds or baby spinach leaves.
- Use prawns or pulled pork instead of chicken.
- Sprinkle with sesame seeds.
- Serve drizzled with sweet chilli sauce or sriracha.

CHAPTER 5

PASTA, RICE & GRAINS

Chicken buckwheat noodles

with peanut butter sauce

SERVES 2
PREP: 10 MINS
COOK: 10 MINS

250g/9oz buckwheat or soba noodles
1 tbsp groundnut oil
225g/8oz chicken breast fillets, cut into strips
4 spring onions, sliced
1 carrot, cut into thin matchsticks
1 red bird's eye chilli, shredded
60g/2oz beansprouts
2 tbsp coarsely chopped peanuts
1 tbsp sesame seeds
a handful of Thai basil or coriander, chopped
lime wedges and sweet chilli sauce, to serve

PEANUT BUTTER SAUCE

60g/2oz peanut butter
2 tbsp soy sauce
1 tbsp water
1 tbsp soft brown sugar or agave or maple syrup
1 tbsp grated fresh ginger
2 garlic cloves, crushed
1 tbsp sesame oil
grated zest and juice of 1 small lime

Soba noodles are made from buckwheat flour and water and are not only delicious but perfect if you are following a gluten-free diet. They have a delightfully nutty, earthy flavour and some 'bite' and are a great partner for spices and aromatics.

1. Make the peanut butter sauce: mix all the ingredients together in a bowl until smooth and well blended. If it's too thick and needs loosening, just add another spoonful of water.

2. Cook the noodles according to the instructions on the packet.

3. Meanwhile, heat the oil in a large frying pan or wok set over a medium to high heat. Add the chicken and stir-fry for 3–4 minutes until golden brown all over. Add the spring onions, carrot and chilli and stir-fry briskly for 1 minute. Stir in the peanut butter sauce, then reduce the heat and cook for 2 minutes.

4. Add the cooked noodles and beansprouts and stir-fry for another 1–2 minutes. Scatter the peanuts over the top and sprinkle with sesame seeds and chopped herbs.

5. Divide between 2 shallow bowls or Food Pots and serve hot or lukewarm with lime wedges and sweet chilli sauce.

OR TRY THIS ...

- Add some shredded spinach or kale.
- Add some sliced red, yellow or green peppers.
- Use cashew or almond butter instead of peanut butter.
- Vegetarians can substitute tofu for the chicken.

Vg

Gochujang tofu *with rice*

The star of this vegan recipe is gochujang, a sweet, slightly smoky and spicy fermented paste that gives the sticky sauce its distinctive flavour. It's important to press the tofu before coating and frying it because it not only contains water but it's also packed in water. Pressing is key to achieving the crispy golden-brown cubes we love to eat.

SERVES 2
PREP: 15 MINS
COOK: 10–15 MINS

115g/4oz long-grain rice (dry weight)
225g/8oz extra-firm tofu, pressed (see note below)
3 tbsp cornflour
2 tbsp vegetable oil
2 tsp sesame seeds
shredded spring onions, for sprinkling
avocado, carrots and cucumber, cut into matchsticks, to serve

STICKY SAUCE

2 tbsp gochujang
1 tbsp soy sauce
1 tbsp Korean rice syrup
2 garlic cloves, crushed
1 tsp grated fresh ginger

NOTE: ***To press the tofu, remove from the packaging and drain well. Cut the block into 4–6 thick slices and place in a single layer between 2 sheets of kitchen paper on a plate. Cover with a clean cloth and put some heavy tins on top. Leave for at least 30 minutes, then drain off the water and pat dry.***

1. Cook the rice according to the instructions on the packet.

2. Meanwhile, cut the tofu into 2.5cm/1in cubes and place in a zip-locked plastic bag with the cornflour. Close the bag and shake gently until all the cubes are well coated. Remove and shake off any excess flour.

3. Make the sticky sauce: put all the ingredients in a small saucepan set over a medium heat and cook, stirring, for 2–3 minutes, or until the sauce starts to bubble and thicken.

4. Heat the oil in frying pan set over a high heat. When it's hot, add the tofu, in batches, and cook, turning occasionally, for 5 minutes, or until crisp and golden brown all over. Remove and drain on kitchen paper, then stir gently into the sticky sauce to coat.

5. Divide the rice between 2 bowls. Arrange the tofu on top and sprinkle with sesame seeds and spring onions. Serve with the avocado, carrot and cucumber matchsticks.

OR TRY THIS ...

- Serve with steamed mangetout or sugar snap peas.
- If you don't have rice syrup, use agave or maple syrup instead.
- Add some tomato ketchup to the sticky sauce.
- Use glutinous rice.

V

Really green spinach risotto

This unusual spinach risotto is a bright emerald green and it's packed with nutrients. For the best results, you need to use a good-quality flavoursome stock (homemade if you have some). It will enhance and enrich the rice, transforming it into a delicious dish. We've given quantities for four servings because it tastes so good served hot, lukewarm, reheated the following day, or rolled into little balls (arancini) and fried in olive oil (see recipe on page 132).

SERVES 4
PREP: 15 MINS
COOK: 30–35 MINS

- 300g/10oz spinach, washed and trimmed
- 45g/1½oz butter
- 3 tbsp olive oil
- 1 large red onion, finely chopped
- 3 garlic cloves, crushed
- 1.2 litres/2 pints vegetable or chicken stock
- 250g/9oz risotto rice, such as carnaroli or arborio
- 120ml/4fl oz white vermouth or dry white wine
- 60g/2oz grated Parmesan cheese, plus extra for sprinkling
- sea salt and black pepper

TIP: ***Be patient – don't be tempted to rush adding the hot stock and slowly stirring the risotto.***

1. Put the spinach leaves in a large colander and pour boiling water over them – enough to make them wilt. When the water drains out and the spinach starts to cool, press down firmly with a saucer to squeeze out any remaining water.

2. Transfer the spinach to a blender or food processor with a small knob of the butter and blitz until you have a bright green purée. Set aside.

3. Heat the remaining butter and olive oil in a large deep frying pan set over a low to medium heat. Cook the onion and garlic, stirring occasionally, for 10 minutes until softened but not coloured.

4. Meanwhile, heat the stock in a large saucepan set over a medium heat. When it starts to simmer, turn the heat down to low.

5. Add the rice to the onion mixture and stir well until all the grains are glistening and so hot that they start to crackle. Quickly pour in the vermouth or wine and cook until the liquid evaporates.

6. Add a ladle of the simmering stock and stir gently until all the liquid is absorbed. Add another ladle and keep doing this, one ladle at a time, stirring frequently, until most or all of the stock has been absorbed and the rice grains are plump and tender but still retain a little 'bite'. They should not be mushy.

7. Remove the pan from the heat and gently stir in the spinach purée, distributing it throughout the risotto. Stir in the grated Parmesan and check the seasoning, adding salt and pepper to taste.

8. Serve the risotto sprinkled with more Parmesan.

OR TRY THIS ...

- Instead of Parmesan, add some crumbled feta or creamy Gorgonzola.
- Fry some chopped celery with the onion and garlic.
- Garnish with crispy pancetta. Dry-fry some rashers until golden brown and crisp. Blot with kitchen paper and crumble over the risotto before serving.

Salmon poke bowl

Unlike Japanese sashimi – thinly sliced raw fish – for Hawaiian poke the fish is cut into cubes and usually marinated in a soy-based sauce then served in a bowl with rice, vegetables or salad. As always, when preparing raw fish, you must take care and use only the best-quality wild-caught salmon available.

SERVES 2
PREP: 15 MINS
COOK: 10–15 MINS

75g/3oz red rice (dry weight)
250g/9oz sushi- or sashimi-grade salmon
2 spring onions, thinly sliced
100g/3½oz frozen edamame beans
¼ cucumber, cut into cubes
4 radishes, thinly sliced
a large handful of baby spinach leaves
shredded nori, to garnish
sesame seeds, for sprinkling

MARINADE

2 tbsp soy sauce
1 tbsp rice vinegar
1 tsp sesame oil
1 tsp sugar or honey

GINGER AND LIME DRESSING

1 tbsp light soy sauce
1 tsp sesame oil
1 tbsp rice vinegar
juice of ½ small lime
1 tsp clear honey
1 tsp grated fresh ginger

1. Cook the rice according to the instructions on the packet.

2. Check the salmon for any small bones, then cut into 2cm/¾in cubes. Place in a bowl with the spring onions.

3. Make the marinade: mix all the ingredients together in a small bowl. Pour over the salmon and stir gently until all the cubes are lightly coated.

4. Blanch the edamame beans in a saucepan of boiling water for 1 minute. Refresh under cold running water and drain well. Place in a salad bowl with the cucumber, radishes and spinach leaves.

5. Make the ginger and lime dressing: mix all the ingredients together in a bowl. Pour over the edamame mixture and toss lightly.

6. Fluff up the grains of rice with a fork and divide between 2 bowls. Add the salmon and the edamame salad, and sprinkle with nori and sesame seeds.

OR TRY THIS ...

- Add some avocado cubes or quartered cherry tomatoes to the salad.
- Use tuna instead of salmon.
- Use white rice, sushi rice or brown rice.
- Garnish with chopped coriander.
- Serve with hot wasabi on the side.

Chipotle chicken bowl

Pulled chicken in a smoky chipotle sauce served with a green quinoa salad makes a lovely summer lunch (or packed lunch). Everything can be made in advance and kept in the fridge until you're ready to eat. If you can get hold of bottled chipotles in adobo sauce, use these instead of chipotle paste for an even more intense flavour.

SERVES 2
PREP: 20 MINS
COOK: 45–55 MINS

300g/10oz chicken breast
200g/7oz tinned chopped tomatoes
1 tbsp tomato purée
2 tbsp chipotle paste
2 garlic cloves, crushed
½ tsp dried oregano
½ tsp ground cumin
1 tsp sugar
1 tbsp lime juice
1 tbsp red wine vinegar
sea salt and black pepper
a few sprigs of coriander, chopped
salsa or pico de gallo, to serve

QUINOA SALAD

300ml/½ pint vegetable stock
115g/4oz quinoa (dry weight)
100g/3½oz mixed greens, such as kale, spinach
3 spring onions, sliced
a small bunch of coriander, chopped
1 small ripe avocado, peeled, stoned and diced
1 garlic clove, crushed
1 green chilli, deseeded and diced
a pinch of sea salt crystals
3 tbsp fruity green olive oil
juice of 1 small lime

1. Put the chicken, tomatoes, tomato purée, chipotle paste, garlic, oregano, cumin and sugar in a saucepan. Add the lime juice and vinegar plus 120ml/4fl oz water. Season with salt and pepper and set the pan over a low to medium heat. Cover with a lid and simmer for 40–50 minutes, stirring occasionally, until the chicken is really tender and the sauce has reduced. Remove the chicken from the pan and shred with 2 forks.

2. Use a stick blender to purée the sauce, then set over a medium heat and let it bubble away for a few minutes until thick.

3. While the chicken is cooking, make the quinoa salad: heat the stock in a saucepan and when it starts to boil, add the quinoa. Reduce the heat, cover the pan and simmer gently for 15 minutes, or until tender and most of the broth has been absorbed. Turn off the heat and leave to steam in the pan for 5–8 minutes. Drain off the excess liquid and fluff up the quinoa with a fork. Set aside to cool a little.

4. Mix together the greens, spring onions, coriander, avocado and warm quinoa in a bowl. Crush the garlic, chilli and sea salt in a pestle and mortar. Gradually stir in the oil and then the lime juice to make a dressing. Stir gently into the quinoa mixture.

5. Divide the quinoa between 2 bowls. Add the shredded chicken with the sauce on the side or stir the chicken into the sauce. Sprinkle with coriander and serve with tomato salsa or pico de gallo.

TIP: ***Instead of cooking the quinoa, you can use a pouch of ready-to-eat cooked quinoa.***

OR TRY THIS ...

- Substitute cooked brown rice or bulgur wheat for the quinoa.
- Serve the chipotle chicken wrapped in tortillas with guacamole (see page 50) and sour cream.
- Use as a filling for quesadillas or pitta pockets.
- Use shredded tinned jackfruit instead of chicken – cook in the sauce in the same way.

V

Thai-style noodle bowl

Crisp, crunchy and refreshing, this aromatic Thai-style salad is really quick and easy to make ... and surprisingly filling. It's very versatile and you can have fun experimenting with different ingredients depending on what you've got in your fridge or kitchen cupboards.

SERVES 2
PREP: 15 MINS

115g (4oz) thin or vermicelli rice noodles (dry weight)
¼ small red cabbage, shredded
1 red pepper, deseeded and thinly sliced
1 large carrot, coarsely grated
¼ cucumber, cut into matchsticks
8 crisp radishes, sliced
4 spring onions, thinly sliced
a few crisp lettuce leaves, torn
a handful of Thai basil, shredded
30g/1oz chopped roasted peanuts
2 tbsp coconut flakes

DRESSING

1 red bird's eye chilli, shredded
2 garlic cloves, thinly sliced
1 tsp grated fresh ginger
2 tbsp nam pla (Thai fish sauce)
1 tbsp rice vinegar
juice of 1 lime
1 tsp caster sugar

1. Cook the rice noodles according to the instructions on the packet. Drain well and cool.

2. Make the dressing: put all the ingredients in a small bowl and whisk together until thoroughly combined.

3. Put the red cabbage, red pepper, carrot, cucumber, radishes, spring onions, lettuce and basil in a large bowl and mix well.

4. Add the rice noodles and gently toss everything in the dressing. Divide between 2 bowls or Food Pots and sprinkle the peanuts and coconut flakes over the top.

OR TRY THIS ...

- To make the salad more substantial, add some prawns, shredded chicken, rare roast beef or griddled tofu.
- For more sweetness, stir in some diced juicy mango or papaya.
- Add a dash of toasted sesame oil to the dressing.

Jerk prawns

This dish is made with kidney beans and creamy coconut milk, infused with allspice berries and Scotch bonnet chillies. If you like jerk seasoning, make four times the quantity and keep what you don't use in a screw-top jar in the fridge for up to 2 weeks. It's perfect for marinating chicken legs and thighs and white fish fillets or even salmon.

SERVES 2
PREP: 15 MINS
MARINATE: 30 MINS
COOK: 20–25 MINS
STAND: 5 MINS

300g/10oz raw shelled large prawns
175g/6oz long-grain rice (dry weight)
240ml/8fl oz tinned coconut milk
180ml/6fl oz water
2 garlic cloves, crushed
2 allspice berries
1 sprig of thyme
1 Scotch bonnet
¼ tsp salt
200g/7oz kidney beans, rinsed and drained
1 tbsp olive oil
a handful of chopped coriander
West Indian hot sauce, to serve

JERK SEASONING

1 tsp allspice berries
1 tsp black peppercorns
a pinch of ground nutmeg
a pinch of cinnamon
leaves from 2 thyme sprigs
1 small shallot, diced
2 garlic cloves, crushed
2.5cm/1in piece of fresh ginger, peeled and diced
1 Scotch bonnet, diced
1 tsp soft brown sugar
2 tsp soy sauce
juice of ½ lime

1. Make the jerk seasoning: crush the allspice berries and peppercorns, then blitz all the ingredients to a paste in a blender. Transfer to a bowl and add the prawns, turning them until coated. Cover and marinate in the fridge for at least 30 minutes.

2. Meanwhile, put the rice in a deep saucepan with the coconut milk, water, garlic, allspice berries, thyme, chilli and salt. Bring to the boil, then add the beans, reduce the heat and cover the pan. Simmer, stirring occasionally to prevent the rice sticking, for 15 minutes, or until all the liquid has been absorbed.

3. Discard the allspice berries, thyme and chilli and leave to stand for 5 minutes, then fluff up the rice with a fork.

4. Heat the oil in a frying pan set over a medium heat and add the prawns (in their jerk marinade). Cook for 1–2 minutes each side until they are pink and succulent. Alternatively, cook them in a hot griddle pan or over hot coals on a barbecue.

5. Serve the prawns with the rice, sprinkled with chopped coriander, with hot sauce on the side for drizzling.

OR TRY THIS ...

- Use black beans instead of kidney beans.
- For the jerk seasoning, use spring onions instead of a shallot.
- For extra sweetness, add some honey to the marinade.

Coconut prawns & rice

SERVES 2
PREP: 15 MINS
MARINATE: 15 MINS
COOK: 20 MINS

This creamy coconut stew (*moqueca de camaroes*) is a popular dish in Brazil where it is usually served with a chilled light beer. Serve, as below, with boiled or steamed rice, or even tossed with linguine or spaghetti.

300g/10oz raw peeled large prawns, deveined
juice of 1 lime
2 tbsp olive oil
1 red onion, finely chopped
3 garlic cloves, crushed
1 large red pepper, deseeded and chopped
1 hot red chilli, deseeded and shredded
3 large juicy tomatoes, coarsely chopped
240ml/8fl oz tinned coconut milk
a handful of coriander, finely chopped, plus extra for garnish
115g/4oz basmati rice (dry weight)
3 spring onions, shredded
sea salt and black pepper
Brazilian hot sauce, such as malagueta pepper sauce, for drizzling
lime wedges, to serve

1. Put the prawns and lime juice in a bowl and leave in the fridge to marinate for 15 minutes.

2. Meanwhile, heat the oil in a large frying pan set over a medium heat. Cook the onion, garlic, pepper and chilli, stirring occasionally, for 8 minutes, or until tender but not coloured.

3. Stir in the tomatoes and cook for 1 minute. Season lightly with salt and pepper, then add the coconut milk and coriander. Reduce the heat and simmer gently for 5 minutes.

4. Add the prawns and cook for 4–5 minutes until they turn pink and the sauce reduces.

5. Meanwhile, cook the rice according to the instructions on the packet.

6. Divide the rice between 2 shallow bowls or Food Pots and ladle the stew over the top. Sprinkle with coriander and spring onions and serve with hot sauce for drizzling and lime wedges for squeezing.

TIP: ***If you can't get the authentic Brazilian hot sauce, you can use Portuguese piri piri or even sriracha or a few drops of Tabasco.***

OR TRY THIS ...

- Add a spoonful of Brazilian hot sauce, sriracha or Tabasco to the stew.
- Use coconut oil instead of olive oil.
- Substitute a tin of chopped tomatoes for the fresh ones.
- Use chunks of firm white fish, such as cod, or defrosted *fruits de mer* instead of prawns.

CHAPTER 6

TARTS, PIES & SLICES

V

Mediterranean filo tart

SERVES 4
PREP: 20 MINS
COOK: 40–50 MINS

A simple summer tart of crispy, flaky filo pastry loaded with roasted vegetables and salty feta. It's easy to make and so versatile – a great way of using up vegetables that are lurking in the back of your fridge.

- 1 aubergine, halved and sliced
- 1 large red onion, cut into thin wedges
- 2 red or yellow peppers, cut into strips
- 2 tbsp olive oil, plus extra for brushing
- a few thyme and rosemary leaves, chopped
- 12 small cherry tomatoes
- 3 large sheets filo pastry
- 100g/3½oz feta cheese, crumbled
- sea salt and black pepper
- chopped flat-leaf parsley, for sprinkling
- good-quality balsamic vinegar, for drizzling

1. Preheat the oven to 200°C, 400°F, gas mark 6. Lightly oil a rectangular 23 x 33cm/9 x 13in loose-bottomed tart tin or a rimmed baking tray.

2. Put the aubergine, onion and peppers in a roasting tin and drizzle with the oil. Sprinkle the herbs over the top and season lightly with salt and pepper.

3. Roast in the oven for 15 minutes, then add the tomatoes to the pan. Return to the oven for a further 10–15 minutes until the vegetables are tender but not mushy.

4. Lightly brush a sheet of filo pastry with oil and place in the oiled tart tin, pushing the pastry into the corners. Repeat with the other 2 sheets of pastry, layering them up. Don't worry if the edges of the pastry hang over the sides – just tuck them in and scrunch them up roughly.

5. Put the roasted vegetables in the tart and sprinkle with the feta. Bake in the oven for 15–20 minutes until the pastry is crisp and golden brown. Sprinkle the parsley over the top.

6. Cut into 4 wedges and serve drizzled with balsamic vinegar with a crisp salad.

TIP: ***Vegans can use a non-dairy cheese instead of feta.***

OR TRY THIS ...

- Spread a little red or green pesto over the pastry base before topping with the roasted vegetables.
- Substitute creamy goat's cheese or slices of chevre for the feta.
- Add some sliced courgettes or fennel bulb.
- Use ready-rolled puff pastry instead of filo.

Mini pissaladiere tarts

MAKES 4
PREP: 15 MINS
COOK: 35–50 MINS

- 2 tbsp olive oil, plus extra for brushing
- 3 large onions, thinly sliced
- 4 large sheets filo pastry
- 80g/3oz tin anchovy fillets, drained
- 16 small black olives, stoned
- sea salt and black pepper

TIP: ***Vegetarians and vegans can substitute strips of roasted red or yellow peppers for the anchovies.***

The classic Provençal pissaladiere is usually made with a pizza-like bread dough in a large rectangular tin. We have used crispy filo pastry for a lighter finish and speedier recipe. The tarts can be made in advance and reheated or eaten cold the following day.

1. Preheat the oven to 190°C, 375°F, gas mark 5. Lightly oil 4 individual 10cm/4in loose-bottomed tartlet tins or 4 large muffin tins.

2. Heat the oil in a large, deep frying pan set over a low heat. Add the onions and cook, stirring occasionally, for 20–30 minutes until the onions are meltingly soft, golden and just starting to caramelise. Season lightly with salt and pepper.

3. Meanwhile, cut a sheet of filo pastry into 8 squares and lightly brush them with oil. Layer them up in a tartlet tin to make a rough star shape – the pastry will come up the sides of the pan to make a 'shell'. Repeat with the other pastry sheets and tins.

4. Divide the onions between the 4 filo shells and make a cross with the anchovies on top of each one. Place an olive in each of the four spaces.

5. Bake in the oven for 15–20 minutes until the pastry is crisp and golden brown. If the filling browns too fast, just cover it with some foil.

6. Serve the tarts hot, lukewarm or even cold. They are best eaten fresh while the filo pastry is still crisp but can be stored in an airtight container in the fridge for up to 48 hours. Reheat them to crisp up the pastry.

OR TRY THIS ...

- Garnish with small rosemary sprigs or add a few chopped leaves to the onions.
- Use red onions instead of white ones.
- Cook 2 crushed garlic cloves with the onions.
- Crumble some feta or goat's cheese over the top.

Vg

Crispy vegan white bean rolls

This is a delicious vegan twist on traditional sausage rolls. Make sure you use a brand of puff pastry that is suitable for vegans – check the label before buying to make sure it does not contain butter or animal fats.

MAKES 16
PREP: 20 MINS
COOK: 35–40 MINS

- 2 tbsp olive oil
- 1 onion, finely chopped
- 3 garlic cloves, crushed
- 1 small red chilli, diced
- 8 sage leaves, finely chopped
- 800g/28oz tinned white beans, such as cannellini or butterbeans, rinsed and drained
- ½ tsp grated nutmeg
- grated zest and juice of ½ lemon
- 350g/12oz ready-rolled puff pastry sheet
- 2 tbsp green pesto
- almond milk, for brushing
- sea salt and black pepper
- tomato chilli jam, to serve (available in some delis and supermarkets)

1. Preheat the oven to 200°C, 400°F, gas mark 6. Line a baking tray with baking parchment.

2. Heat the oil in a saucepan set over a low heat and cook the onion, garlic and chilli, stirring occasionally, for 8–10 minutes until softened but not coloured.

3. Stir in the sage and cook for 1 minute, then add the beans, nutmeg and lemon zest. Cook for 5 minutes until everything is warmed through. Add the lemon juice and seasoning to taste. Mash everything coarsely with a potato masher.

4. Cut the puff pastry sheet in half lengthways into 2 rectangles. Lightly brush each one with the pesto, leaving a small border around the edge.

5. Divide the white bean mixture into 2 portions and shape each one into a long cylinder. Place one, a little way in from the edge, on the long side of each pastry rectangle. Dampen one long edge of each rectangle with almond milk, then fold the other long edge over the filling and roll up to completely enclose it, ending up with the join underneath.

6. Slice each roll into 8 pieces, approximately 4cm/1in long. Brush each one with almond milk and arrange them on the lined baking sheet.

7. Bake in the oven for 20–25 minutes until puffed up, crisp and golden brown. Serve hot or cold with tomato chilli jam.

OR TRY THIS ...

- Serve with tomato ketchup or some hot sauce.
- Instead of green pesto, spread with red pesto or even some Thai curry paste.

Vg

SERVES 6
PREP: 30 MINS
COOK: 1–1¼ HOURS

Vegan coiled spanakopita

A vegan version of the classic spanakopita is eaten throughout Greece during Lent. Here the spinach filling is rolled up inside the filo pastry in a coiled spiral shape (like a Catherine wheel).

1kg/2lb 4oz spinach, washed, trimmed and hard stalks removed
4 tbsp olive oil, plus extra for brushing
3 large leeks, chopped
1 onion, finely chopped
2 garlic cloves, crushed
a bunch of spring onions, thinly sliced
a bunch of dill, finely chopped
a handful of flat-leaf parsley, finely chopped
½ tsp freshly grated nutmeg
a good squeeze of lemon juice
400g/14oz pack filo pastry
sea salt and black pepper

1. Preheat the oven to 190°C, 375°F, gas mark 5.

2. Put the spinach leaves in a large saucepan set over a high heat. Cover the pan and cook, shaking occasionally, for 3–4 minutes, or until the spinach wilts and softens. Drain in a colander, pressing down with a saucer to squeeze out excess moisture. Chop the spinach coarsely.

3. Heat the olive oil in a large frying pan set over a low to medium heat and cook the leeks and onion for 8–10 minutes, or until tender. Stir in the garlic and spring onions and cook for 2–3 minutes, then add the herbs and spinach. Stir in the nutmeg and lemon juice and season to taste with salt and pepper. Turn off the heat and set aside to cool.

4. Unroll the filo pastry and spread out a large sheet on a clean work surface. Only remove the sheets one at a time, as and when you need them, and keep the unused sheets covered with a damp tea towel to stop them drying out. Lightly brush the filo sheet with olive oil and place another sheet on top. Continue layering the sheets in this way, brushing each one with oil, until they are all used up.

5. Shape the spinach mixture into a long, thick cylinder and place along one long side of the filo pastry rectangle, leaving a 2.5cm/1in border along the edge. Fold the pastry over the filling and then roll up like a cigar until you have a stuffed long cylinder.

6. Place it, seam-side down, on the work surface. Coil it into a spiral shape (like a snail), brushing it with oil as you go, so the coils stick together.

7. Lift it carefully and place on a lightly oiled baking sheet. Brush the top with more oil and bake in the oven for 45–50 minutes, or until the pastry is crisp and golden brown.

8. Leave to cool a little before cutting into wedges to serve. Eat hot, lukewarm or cold with some salad.

TIP: ***If you're not a vegan, you can add 225g/8oz crumbled feta cheese and 1 beaten egg to the spinach mixture for a more traditional pie filling.***

OR TRY THIS ...

- Mix in some Swiss chard, kale or spring greens.
- Add some crushed red chilli flakes.
- Add some crumbled vegan cheese to the filling.

V

Cheesy butternut & spinach tortilla wedges

SERVES 4
PREP: 15 MINS
COOK: 25–35 MINS

This Spanish-style tortilla is best eaten lukewarm or at room temperature. It makes an easy supper or brunch and it's perfect for a picnic or packed lunch. Any leftovers can be put in an airtight container and taken to work the following day.

500g/1lb 2oz butternut squash, peeled and cubed
3 tbsp olive oil
1 large red onion, finely chopped
2 red peppers, deseeded and cut into thin strips
3 garlic cloves, crushed
1 tsp smoked paprika
1 red chilli, deseeded and diced
200g/7oz spinach, washed, trimmed and shredded
6 medium free-range eggs
60ml/2fl oz milk
60g/2oz grated Manchego cheese
sea salt and black pepper

1. Cook the butternut squash in a saucepan of boiling water for 6–8 minutes, or until just tender but still holding its shape and it has a little bite. Drain well and set aside.

2. Heat the oil in a large non-stick frying pan set over a low to medium heat. Cook the onion, red peppers and garlic, stirring occasionally, for 8–10 minutes until softened but not browned. Stir in the smoked paprika, then add the chilli, butternut squash and spinach. Cook for 3–4 minutes, stirring occasionally, until the spinach wilts.

3. Beat the eggs and milk together in a bowl and season lightly with salt and pepper. Pour into the pan and reduce the heat to a simmer. Cook gently for 5–10 minutes, or until the tortilla is set and golden brown underneath but still with a little liquid on top.

4. Sprinkle with the Manchego and pop the pan under a preheated hot grill for 5 minutes, or until the tortilla is set and lightly browned on top.

5. Slide the cooked tortilla out of the pan onto a wooden board and leave it to cool for 5–10 minutes. When it's lukewarm, cut into wedges and serve with a crisp salad.

OR TRY THIS …

- Substitute pumpkin or sweet potato for the squash.
- Add some kale, spring greens or watercress.
- If you don't have Manchego, use Cheddar or even diced goat's cheese.
- For extra spice, add some diced chorizo.

CHAPTER 7

SNACKS & TREATS

Vg

Sesame chia seed balls

These bite-sized energy balls are mini power snacks to keep in the fridge or freezer or to take with you to work or out on a bike ride or park run. They are nutrient-dense, providing you with protein as well as a jackpot of minerals: zinc, copper, iron, magnesium and phosphorous. Vegans can substitute agave or maple syrup for the honey.

MAKES APPROX. 30 BALLS
PREP: 15 MINS
CHILL: 1–2 HOURS

- 175g/6oz peanut butter
- 6 tbsp clear honey
- 175g/6oz porridge oats
- 30g/1oz chia seeds
- 30g/1oz dried blueberries or cranberries
- 60g/2oz dark chocolate chips (minimum 70% cocoa solids)
- 2 tbsp sesame seeds

1. Put the peanut butter and honey in a saucepan over a low heat and stir gently until just warm and well blended.

2. Remove from the heat and stir in the oats, seeds, dried fruit and chocolate chips, distributing them evenly throughout the mixture. If it's too sticky and wet, add some more oats; if it's too dry, stir in a little cold water.

3. Take small spoonfuls of the mixture and, with your hands, mould them into small balls. Roll them in the sesame seeds to evenly coat them.

4. Place on a large baking tray lined with baking parchment and chill in the fridge for 1–2 hours until set firm. Transfer to an airtight container and store in the fridge for up to 10 days.

TIP: ***Use a microwave to blend the peanut butter and honey.***

OR TRY THIS …

- Roll the balls in shredded unsweetened coconut or finely chopped walnuts.
- Use almond or cashew butter instead of peanut butter.
- Blitz some dates to a sticky paste and substitute for some of the nut butter.
- Add some pumpkin, flax, sunflower or poppy seeds.
- Add some finely chopped nuts, such as roasted cashews.

V

Mango matcha chia power pots

Chia seeds are packed with a hefty punch of plant protein and other nutrients. Overnight they swell to thicken the coconut milk – they can swell up to 10 times their original size when soaked, acquiring a gel-like consistency.

SERVES 2
PREP: 15 MINS
CHILL: OVERNIGHT

- 4 tbsp chia seeds
- 240ml/8fl oz coconut milk
- 1 level tsp matcha powder
- 1 tsp agave syrup
- 1 small ripe mango, peeled, stoned and diced
- 2 tbsp dairy-free coconut yoghurt
- a few strawberries, raspberries or blueberries, for topping
- 2 tbsp chopped hazelnuts or pistachios

1. Put the chia seeds and coconut milk in a bowl and whisk together.

2. In another bowl, blend the matcha powder and agave syrup until evenly mixed, then stir into the chia mixture with the diced mango.

3. Divide the mixture between 2 bowls, screw-top jam jars or Food Pots and cover with some cling film.

4. Chill in the fridge overnight, or until all the liquid is absorbed and the mixture has a jelly-like texture.

5. The following day, top each pot with a spoonful of yoghurt and then sprinkle with the berries and nuts. If you've used Food Pots, cover with the lids and take them with you to work or college.

OR TRY THIS …

- Use diced peach, nectarine, cherries or plums instead of mango.
- Use clear honey or maple syrup instead of agave.
- Add a dash of vanilla extract or the scraped-out seeds of a vanilla pod to the chia mixture.
- Substitute almond milk for the coconut milk, and top with Greek yoghurt.

Vg

MAKES 8
PREP: 20 MINS
COOK: 5 MINS

Fresh rice paper rolls

These delicious spring rolls are much fresher-tasting, lighter and healthier than fried ones. You can buy rice paper wrappers in oriental stores, delis and many supermarkets.

60g/2oz rice vermicelli noodles (dry weight)
1 tsp sesame oil
100g/3½oz shredded greens or red cabbage
1 large red pepper, deseeded and cut into thin strips
1 large carrot, cut into small thin matchsticks
85g/3oz beansprouts
4 spring onions, shredded
¼ cucumber, cut into thin matchsticks
a large handful of coriander, chopped
1 tsp grated fresh ginger
2 tbsp soy sauce
juice of ½ lime
8 round rice paper wrappers

PEANUT DIPPING SAUCE

100g/3½oz peanut butter
2 garlic cloves, crushed
2 tbsp sweet chilli sauce
juice of ½ lime
2 tbsp soy sauce
1 tbsp toasted sesame oil
3–4 tbsp water

1. Make the peanut dipping sauce: whisk the peanut butter, garlic, sweet chilli sauce, lime juice, soy sauce and sesame oil in a bowl until well combined. Add the water, a tablespoon at a time, until smooth and creamy. Set aside while you make the spring rolls.

2. Cook the rice noodles according to the instructions on the packet. Drain well and rinse under running cold water. Pat dry and toss in the sesame oil.

3. Put all the prepared vegetables in a bowl with the coriander, ginger, soy sauce and lime juice and toss lightly.

4. Fill a bowl with cold water and position it near you while you assemble the spring rolls.

5. Dip a rice paper wrapper into the water until it's pliable. Lay it out flat on a clean work surface and add a few rice noodles followed by some of the mixed vegetables, leaving a broad edge around them.

6. Fold the sides of the wrapper over the filling to enclose it and then roll up like a parcel or burrito. Repeat with the rest of the wrappers, rice noodles and vegetable filling.

7. Serve the spring rolls as snacks or appetisers with the peanut dipping sauce.

OR TRY THIS ...

- Instead of coriander, use Thai basil or mint.
- Substitute nam pla (Thai fish sauce) for the soy sauce.
- Add a ripe mango, peeled, stoned and cut into strips.
- Add some sliced radishes or mooli or even some diced avocado.
- Add some cooked prawns or chicken.

Spring green samosas

MAKES 8
PREP: 30 MINS
COOK: 35–40 MINS

These spicy savoury pastries can be served hot or cold. Baking them rather than frying them makes them less oily and more healthy.

- 450g/1lb potatoes, peeled and cubed
- 1 tbsp sunflower oil, plus extra for brushing
- a bunch of spring onions, thinly sliced
- 2 garlic cloves, crushed
- 1 green chilli, diced
- 1 tsp grated fresh ginger
- 2 tsp nigella seeds
- 1 tsp ground cumin
- 1 tsp ground turmeric
- 1 tsp garam masala
- 1 tbsp curry paste
- 250g/9oz spring greens or spinach, trimmed and shredded
- 2 tbsp water
- a handful of mint, chopped
- a squeeze of lime juice
- 8 sheets filo pastry
- sea salt and black pepper
- lime pickle or mango chutney, to serve

1. Preheat the oven to 200°C, 400°F, gas mark 6. Line a baking tray with baking parchment.

2. Boil or steam the potatoes for 8–10 minutes, or until just tender – they should still be a little firm and keep their shape. Drain well.

3. Meanwhile, heat the oil in a saucepan set over a low heat and cook the spring onions and garlic, stirring occasionally, for 2–3 minutes until softened. Add the chilli, ginger, seeds and ground spices and cook for 2 minutes. Stir in the curry paste and cook for 1 minute.

4. Add the greens and water and cook for 2 minutes until they wilt. Gently stir in the cooked potato, mint and lime juice. Check the seasoning, adding salt and pepper if needed, and leave to cool.

5. Place one sheet of filo pastry on a clean work surface and brush lightly with oil. Cover with another sheet and brush with oil. Cut lengthways down the middle into 2 long rectangles.

6. Put a spoonful of the cooled sweet potato mixture into the top right-hand corner of each strip of pastry. Fold the pastry over the filling at an angle to make a triangle, then keep on folding it over until you get to the bottom of each strip. You should end up with a neat triangular pastry parcel enclosing the filling. Repeat with the remaining sheets of filo pastry and the potato mixture to make 8 samosas.

7. Brush the samosas lightly with oil and place them on the lined baking tray. Cook in the oven for 25 minutes until crisp and golden. Serve warm or cold with lime pickle or mango chutney.

OR TRY THIS…

- Use black mustard, crushed coriander or cumin seeds.
- Substitute frozen peas for the greens.
- Add a little coconut cream.
- Serve the samosas with hot sauce for drizzling or dipping.

V

Curried jackfruit samosas

with mango salsa

MAKES 8
PREP: 40 MINS
COOK: 30–35 MINS

- 450g/1lb sweet potatoes, peeled and cubed
- 1 tbsp sunflower oil, plus extra for brushing
- 1 onion, finely chopped
- 2 garlic cloves, crushed
- 1 red chilli, diced
- 1 tsp grated fresh ginger
- 2 tsp black mustard seeds
- 1 tbsp curry paste
- 400g/14oz tin green jackfruit, drained and shredded with a fork
- 200g/7oz baby spinach leaves
- 2 tbsp water
- a handful of coriander, chopped
- 8 sheets filo pastry

MANGO SALSA

- 1 large ripe mango, peeled, stoned and diced
- 1 red pepper, deseeded and diced
- ½ red onion, finely chopped
- 1–2 red chillies, diced
- a large handful of coriander, chopped
- juice of 1 lime
- sea salt flakes, to taste

Jackfruit is the healthy fruit with the 'meaty' texture that has become the number one ethical alternative to meat. It's perfect in these crisp and spicy samosas.

1. Make the mango salsa: mix everything together in a bowl, adding salt to taste. Cover and set aside while you make the samosas.

2. Preheat the oven to 200°C, 400°F, gas mark 6. Line a baking tray with baking parchment.

3. Boil the potatoes for 10 minutes, or until just tender but not mushy – they should keep their shape. Drain well.

4. Meanwhile, heat the oil in a pan set over a low heat and cook the onion and garlic, stirring until softened. Add the chilli, ginger and mustard seeds and cook until the seeds pop. Stir in the curry paste and cook for 1 minute.

5. Add the jackfruit, spinach and water and cook for 5 minutes. Stir in the cooked sweet potato and seasoning to taste. Set aside to cool.

6. Place one sheet of filo pastry on a clean work surface and brush lightly with oil. Cover with another sheet and brush with oil. Cut lengthways down the middle into 2 long rectangles.

7. Place a spoonful of the cooled curry mixture on the top right-hand corner of each strip of pastry. Fold the pastry over the filling at an angle to make a triangle, then keep on folding it over until you get to the bottom of each strip. You should end up with a neat triangular pastry parcel enclosing the filling. Repeat to make 8 samosas.

8. Brush the samosas lightly with oil and place on the lined baking tray. Cook in the oven for 20–25 minutes until crisp and golden. Serve warm with the mango salsa.

OR TRY THIS ...

- Use pumpkin or squash instead of sweet potato.
- Add cumin seeds or ground turmeric to the filling.

V

Chilli cheese nachos

SERVES 4
PREP: 10 MINS
COOK: 10 MINS

- 225g/8oz salted corn tortilla chips
- 4 ripe tomatoes, deseeded and diced
- 400g/14oz tin kidney beans, rinsed and drained
- a bunch of spring onions, finely sliced
- 4 pickled jalapenos, thinly sliced
- 100g/3½oz grated Cheddar or Monterey Jack cheese
- 150g/5oz guacamole (see page 50)
- 150g/5oz hot salsa or pico de gallo
- sour cream or Greek yoghurt, to serve

Nachos are so versatile – they make a tasty snack or are the perfect accompaniment to pre-dinner drinks. They're so simple and speedy to make.

1. Preheat the oven to 200°C, 400°F, gas mark 6.

2. Put the tortilla chips in a large ovenproof dish and scatter the tomatoes, kidney beans, spring onions and jalapenos over the top. Sprinkle with the grated cheese.

3. Bake in the oven for 10 minutes, or until everything is hot and the cheese melts and bubbles.

4. Spoon the guacamole and salsa or pico de gallo over the top and serve with sour cream or yoghurt.

OR TRY THIS ...

- Instead of pickled jalapenos, use 2 sliced hot red or green chillies.
- Use tinned black beans instead of kidney beans.
- Sprinkle with chopped coriander.
- Drizzle with hot sauce.
- Substitute the guacamole with diced avocado tossed in lime juice.

OR TRY THIS …

- Use olive oil instead of melted butter for brushing the filo pastry.
- Substitute finely chopped shallots for the spring onions.
- For a less salty filling, use ricotta instead of feta.

V

Spanakopita filo sticks

These crisp filo sticks filled with spinach and feta cream are a variation on the traditional Greek spinach pie. Eat them as snacks or dippers or serve them for a light meal with a salad.

MAKES APPROX. 32
PREP: 30 MINS
COOK: 15–20 MINS

- 2 tsp olive oil
- a bunch of spring onions, thinly sliced
- 2 garlic cloves, crushed
- 400g/14oz spinach
- 100g/3½oz feta cheese, crumbled
- a handful of dill, finely chopped
- 4 sheets filo pastry
- 60g/2oz unsalted butter
- 3 tbsp white sesame seeds
- sea salt and black pepper

1. Preheat the oven to 180°C, 350°F, gas mark 4. Line 2 baking trays with baking parchment.

2. Heat the oil in a pan set over a low heat and gently cook the spring onions and garlic for 4–5 minutes until tender.

3. Wash the spinach well, removing any thick stalks. Place the leaves in a colander and pour boiling water over them until they wilt. Drain, then press down with a saucer to squeeze out any excess water.

4. Chop the spinach and place in a bowl with the spring onions, feta and dill. Mix together gently, then season to taste with salt and pepper.

5. Place the sheets of filo pastry on a clean work surface or board and cut each one in half lengthways into 2 rectangles. Cut each of these rectangles into 4, so you end up with 8 rectangles from each sheet.

6. Melt the butter in a small pan set over a low heat and brush lightly over one of the pastry rectangles. Smear a little of the spinach filling along the long side of the rectangle, leaving a small edge, then roll up tightly like a cigar. Place, seam-side down, on a lined baking tray. Repeat with the other filo rectangles in the same way.

7. Brush lightly with the remaining melted butter and sprinkle with sesame seeds. Bake in the oven for 12–15 minutes until crisp and golden brown. Remove and eat warm or cold.

V

MAKES APPROX. 12
PREP: 15 MINS
COOK (FROM SCRATCH): 25–30 MINS
COOK (USING LEFTOVER RISOTTO): 10–15 MINS

Lemon, dill & mozzarella arancini

Crisp and golden fried balls of creamy risotto are a Sicilian favourite and have become a popular street food in Italy. You can use any cold risotto, including the spinach one in this book, or make the arancini from scratch.

- 1 quantity cooked spinach risotto (see page 100)

OR

- 720ml/24fl oz vegetable or chicken stock
- ¼ tsp sea salt
- a few saffron strands
- 250g/9oz risotto rice, such as carnaroli or arborio
- grated zest of 1 lemon
- a bunch of dill, finely chopped
- 60g/2oz grated Parmesan cheese

AND

- sunflower oil, for deep-frying
- sea salt flakes and lemon wedges, to serve

FILLING AND COATING

- 200g/7oz mozzarella, cut into 12 cubes
- 1 medium egg, beaten
- 175g/6oz plain flour
- 250g/9oz dried breadcrumbs

TIP: ***You could make smaller balls, moulding the rice around diced mozzarella, and shallow-fry them.***

1. If you don't have any cooked or leftover risotto, put the stock, salt and saffron in a large saucepan set over a high heat and bring to the boil. Add the rice and when the water comes back to the boil, reduce the heat and simmer gently for 15 minutes, or until the liquid has been absorbed and the rice is tender but not mushy – it should still have some 'bite'.

2. Stir in the lemon zest, dill and grated Parmesan, then check the seasoning, adding more salt if necessary. Transfer to a bowl and leave until cold before covering and further chilling the rice in the fridge.

3. When the rice is completely cold (or use the cold leftover spinach risotto), take heaped tablespoons of the mixture and, using your hands, roll each one around a cube of mozzarella to make a ball. You should end up with approximately 12 balls. Dampen your hands with a little water to make this easier.

4. Put the beaten egg and flour in a bowl with some cold water – about 150ml/5fl oz – and beat to a thick batter. Dip the arancini balls into the batter and then roll them in the breadcrumbs until coated all over.

5. Heat the oil in a deep heavy-based saucepan or deep-fat fryer to 170°C/325°F. If you don't have a sugar thermometer to measure this, test it by dropping in a few breadcrumbs. If they sizzle and float, the oil is ready.

6. Fry the arancini in batches, taking care not to overcrowd the pan, for 4–5 minutes, or until crisp and golden all over. Remove with a slotted spoon and drain on kitchen paper.

7. Serve sprinkled with salt with lemon wedges, for squeezing. The arancini are also delicious cold.

Santorini fava
with pitta triangles

V

SERVES 8
PREP: 15 MINS
COOK: 1 HOUR

Traditionally, fava was made with dried fava beans, but yellow split peas are now more commonly used. Serve as a meze dish, an appetiser or as a dip (as below).

- 450g/1lb yellow split peas (dry weight)
- 1 onion, quartered
- 2 garlic cloves, peeled
- 1 bay leaf
- a few sprigs of thyme
- 100ml/3½fl oz olive oil, plus extra for drizzling
- juice of 1 lemon
- sea salt and black pepper
- pitta breads or flatbreads

CARAMELISED ONION TOPPING

- 4 tbsp olive oil
- 3 red onions, thinly sliced
- a pinch of sugar
- 2–3 tbsp red wine vinegar

1. Rinse the split peas in a sieve under running cold water. Put them into a large saucepan with the onion, garlic and herbs. Cover with plenty of cold water and set over a high heat. Bring to the boil and skim off the foamy scum that rises to the surface.

2. Lower the heat and simmer gently for 40–50 minutes, or until the split peas are very soft and most of the water has been absorbed. Drain in a sieve suspended over a bowl to catch the cooking liquid. Discard the onion and herbs but keep the garlic.

3. Meanwhile, make the caramelised onion topping: heat the oil in a frying pan over a low heat. Add the onions and cook, stirring occasionally, for 15 minutes, or until tender and golden brown. Stir in the sugar and vinegar and cook for 5–10 minutes until the onions are sticky and starting to caramelise. Season to taste with salt and pepper.

4. Put the split peas and garlic in a blender or food processor. With the motor running, start adding the olive oil through the feed tube in a thin steady stream, then add the lemon juice. If the mixture is too thick, add some of the reserved cooking liquid or more lemon juice. Season to taste with salt and pepper.

5. Spoon into a serving bowl and drizzle with olive oil. Serve lukewarm or cold topped with the caramelised onions. Cut the pitta or flatbreads into triangles and heat in a griddle pan, then use as dippers. The fava keeps in an airtight container in the fridge for up to 4 days.

TIP: ***For a coarser chunky texture, use a potato masher instead of blitzing the split peas in a blender or food processor.***

OR TRY THIS ...

- Instead of caramelised onions, sprinkle with diced red onion and capers.
- Dust with paprika or cayenne.
- Use balsamic vinegar instead of red wine in the caramelised onions.

Curried chicken roti

Rotis are thin, round flatbreads that originated in India and have now become a popular street food in the Caribbean, especially Trinidad and Tobago. They are usually wrapped around a filling of curried or jerked meat (chicken or goat), spicy chickpeas or conch, and served with a fiery hot sauce.

SERVES 4
PREP: 30 MINS
REST: 1 HOUR
COOK: 45 MINS

225g/8oz self-raising flour, sifted
¼ tsp ground turmeric
½ tsp salt
1 tbsp sunflower oil, plus extra for brushing and frying
120ml/4fl oz tepid water
West Indian hot sauce, for drizzling

CURRIED CHICKEN FILLING

2 tbsp sunflower oil
1 onion, finely chopped
2 garlic cloves, crushed
1 small butternut squash, peeled and diced
300g/10oz chicken breast fillets, diced
1 tbsp curry powder
1 tsp paprika
a pinch of ground allspice
120ml/4fl oz coconut milk
100g/3½oz baby spinach leaves
sea salt and black pepper

1. Make the roti dough: put the flour, turmeric and salt in a mixing bowl and drizzle the oil over the top. Mix in the water, a little at a time, until you have a soft dough. If it's too dry, add a little more water.

2. Knead the dough lightly for a few minutes, then cover and set aside to rest for at least 30 minutes.

3. Divide into 8 equal-sized pieces and roll each one out into a thin circle. Lightly brush half of each circle with oil and fold over. Brush half of the semicircle with oil and fold over again. Set aside for 30 minutes.

4. Meanwhile, make the curried chicken filling: heat the oil in a heavy-based frying pan and cook the onion and garlic over a low to medium heat for 5 minutes. Add the squash and chicken and cook for 5 minutes, stirring occasionally, until the chicken is browned all over. Stir in the curry powder and spices.

5. Add the coconut milk and simmer for 15 minutes, or until the chicken is cooked through, the vegetables are tender and the liquid has evaporated. A couple of minutes before the end of the cooking time, stir in the spinach and season to taste.

6. Roll out the roti into thin circles and fry, one at a time, in a little hot oil in a frying pan for 2 minutes until golden brown underneath and slightly puffy, then flip them over and cook the other side. Drain on kitchen paper and keep warm.

7. Divide the curried chicken between the roti pancakes and fold over or roll up. Serve drizzled with West Indian hot sauce.

OR TRY THIS ...

- Use pumpkin instead of squash.
- Substitute black beans, prawns, pork or minced beef for the chicken.
- Use curry paste instead of curry powder.

TIP: ***Many West Indian hot sauces are available online.***

CHAPTER 8

DRINKS

V

On-the-go breakfast smoothie

There's no excuse for skipping breakfast, even if you're in a rush to leave home in the morning. It only takes 5 minutes to throw some healthy fruit, oats and cinnamon into a blender and decant into a Chilly's Bottle or Cup to enjoy a colourful smoothie on the go.

SERVES 2
PREP: 5 MINS

4 tbsp rolled oats
100g/3½oz blueberries
100g/3½oz raspberries
1 frozen large banana (see note on page 17)
240ml/8fl oz oat milk
240ml/8fl oz coconut milk
a good pinch of ground cinnamon

1. Tip the oats into a blender and pulse to grind them.

2. Add the berries, frozen banana, milks and cinnamon, then blitz until smooth and creamy.

3. Pour into 2 glasses or Chilly's Bottles to serve.

OR TRY THIS ...

- You don't have to use a frozen banana – use a ripe one instead.
- Vary the berries: try strawberries or blackberries.
- Use any plant milk, such as almond, hazelnut or soya.
- Flavour with vanilla extract instead of cinnamon.
- For extra sweetness, add some maple syrup or agave.

Vg

Almond vanilla smoothie

SERVES 2
PREP: 5 MINS

4 tbsp almond butter
2 tsp ground flaxseed
2 frozen medium bananas (see note on page 17)
240ml/8fl oz almond milk or vanilla soy milk
240g/8oz vanilla or Greek yoghurt
a few drops of vanilla extract
1–2 tsp clear honey (optional)
a few chia seeds, for sprinkling

This makes a delicious pick-me-up at any time of day, as well as a quick breakfast. If you're vegan, use non-dairy yoghurt and sweeten with maple or agave syrup instead of honey.

1. Put all the ingredients in a blender and blitz until thick and smooth.

2. Pour into 2 tall glasses or Chilly's Bottles, sprinkle with the chia seeds and enjoy.

OR TRY THIS ...

- Use peanut or cashew butter.
- Add some chopped dates, berries or hemp powder.
- Substitute almond extract for vanilla extract.

V

Matcha latte

Matcha and coconut are a flavour combo made in heaven, and the colour of this latte is so beautiful. You don't have to make it in mugs – use a large jug instead and then decant into your Chilly's Bottle or Cup for a latte on the go.

SERVES 2
PREP: 10 MINS

1 tsp matcha powder, sifted
150ml/5fl oz just-boiled water
a good pinch of ground cinnamon
a pinch of grated nutmeg
240ml/8fl oz coconut milk
honey, stevia, agave or maple syrup, to taste

1. Take 2 mugs and put ½ teaspoon matcha in each one. Add the just-boiled water and whisk well until the matcha has dissolved and there are no lumps. Whisk in the ground spices. You can use a small, hand-held electric whisk to do this.

2. Heat the coconut milk and divide between the 2 mugs. Whisk again until frothy and foamy. Sweeten to taste with whichever sweetener you prefer.

TIP: ***You don't have to sift the matcha powder but it does prevent it clumping and makes the latte smoother and easier to whisk.***

OR TRY THIS ...

- Make the latte with almond, hazelnut or oat milk.
- Add a few drops of vanilla extract.
- Use reduced-fat coconut milk instead of full-fat.
- Omit the spices and whisk in some melted white chocolate chips and vanilla extract.

V

Golden milk

This warmly spiced turmeric and coconut milk latte is relaxing and comforting at any time of day. We've used reduced-fat tinned coconut milk but you can substitute the full-fat type if you prefer a creamier, richer latte.

SERVES 2
PREP: 5 MINS
COOK: 5–10 MINS

- 480ml/16fl oz reduced-fat tinned coconut milk
- 2 tsp ground turmeric
- 2 tsp finely grated fresh ginger
- freshly ground black pepper
- 1 cinnamon stick
- 4 cardamom pods, crushed
- a pinch of freshly grated nutmeg
- stevia, to taste

1. Whisk the coconut milk, turmeric, ginger and a grinding of black pepper until well combined and frothy.

2. Pour into a saucepan and add the cinnamon stick and crushed cardamom pods. Bring to the boil, then reduce the heat to low to medium and simmer gently for 5 minutes, whisking once or twice.

3. Remove from the heat and sweeten to taste with stevia. Strain through a sieve or fine-mesh strainer into 2 mugs or Chilly's Bottles.

TIP: ***Add 1 teaspoon of coconut oil to make it easier for your body to absorb the turmeric.***

OR TRY THIS ...

- Use unsweetened almond milk instead of coconut milk.
- Stir in the scraped-out seeds of ½ vanilla pod.
- Add a star anise or a pinch of Chinese five spice powder or cayenne.
- Use ground ginger instead of fresh for a milder, more subtle flavour.

V

Iced tea

Nothing is more refreshing than iced tea on a hot summer's day. We've got a traditional recipe flavoured with lemon, plus a real treat: a sparkling green matcha version.

Lemon iced tea

SERVES 4
PREP: 10 MINS

960ml/32fl oz boiling water (from a kettle)
4 black tea bags
1 tbsp sugar
2 lemons, sliced
ice cubes and mint sprigs, to serve

1. Fill a kettle and put on to boil. Meanwhile, put the tea bags, sugar and 1 sliced lemon in a large heatproof jug. Pour over the boiling water and set aside for 5 minutes.

2. Remove and discard the tea bags and sliced lemon. Leave the tea to cool.

3. Cover and chill in the fridge for up to 3 days. To serve, pour the chilled tea over some ice cubes in a glass and add a slice of lemon and a sprig of mint.

TIP: ***Experiment with different tea bags, such as Earl Grey or lapsang souchong.***

Matcha mint iced tea

SERVES 1
PREP: 5 MINS

200ml/7fl oz sparkling water
½ tsp matcha powder
juice of ½ lime
a handful of mint leaves, plus a sprig to serve
a squeeze of clear honey or agave syrup
ice cubes and lime slices, to serve

1. Pour the water into a blender and add the matcha powder, lime juice, mint and honey or agave.

2. Blitz until well blended and smooth. Check that the drink is sweetened to your taste, adding more honey or agave, if wished.

3. Pour over ice cubes, add some lime slices and enjoy.

V

Iced coffee

There are so many ways of making iced coffee. The shakerato is a popular drink throughout Italy in the summer months and is strictly for espresso afficionados, whereas the iced coffee latte will appeal to milky coffee lovers.

Shakerato

SERVES 1
PREP: 5 MINS

45ml/1½fl oz freshly brewed espresso or very strong coffee, cooled slightly
1 tbsp full-fat milk
1 tsp sugar syrup
5 ice cubes, plus extra for serving

1. Put the coffee, milk and sugar syrup in a cocktail shaker. Add the ice and seal.

2. Shake vigorously for 20–30 seconds, or until the coffee is chilled and frothy.

3. Pour the iced coffee through a slotted spoon or strainer into a glass or Chilly's Coffee Cup filled with ice cubes.

Iced coffee latte

SERVES 1
PREP: 5 MINS

60ml/2fl oz freshly brewed espresso or really strong coffee
2 tsp maple syrup or soft brown sugar
ice cubes
100ml/3½fl oz cold full-fat milk
whipped cream, to serve (optional)

1. Mix the coffee and maple syrup or sugar – if using sugar, make sure it dissolves.

2. Fill a glass or Chilly's Bottle with ice and add the sweetened espresso.

3. Put the milk in a screw-top glass jar and seal tightly. Shake vigorously until it's very frothy.

4. Pour the milk into the iced espresso and enjoy! If wished, top with whipped cream.

TIP: ***For a vanilla version use vanilla sugar syrup or add a few drops of vanilla extract.***

Bone broth
with tofu & seaweed

We've used a richly flavoured chicken bone broth in this healthy, immunity-boosting hot drink and given it an umami twist. Making your own bone broth at home takes a little time but it's well worth the effort. It freezes well, too, so you can decant it into smaller portions to freeze and reheat for soups and drinks. You can make a richer, darker broth with roasted beef marrow bones, but it will take 12–24 hours to simmer.

SERVES 2
PREP: 10 MINS
COOK: 1¼ HOURS
CHILL: OVERNIGHT
REHEAT: 10 MINS

- a few pieces of dried nori or wakame seaweed, crumbled
- 1 tbsp white miso paste
- 3 spring onions, thinly sliced
- 1 garlic clove, crushed
- 6 thin asparagus stems, cut into 1cm/½in lengths
- 100g/3½oz firm tofu, diced
- dried crushed chilli flakes and chopped coriander, for sprinkling (optional)

CHICKEN BONE BROTH

- 2 chicken carcasses
- 2 red onions, peeled and quartered
- 1 leek, washed, trimmed and sliced
- 1 celery stick, sliced
- 1 carrot, sliced
- 2 garlic cloves, sliced
- 2 bay leaves
- a few sprigs of thyme
- a handful of parsley
- 1 tsp whole black peppercorns
- 2.25 litres/4 pints water
- sea salt, to taste

1. Make the chicken broth: put the chicken carcasses in a large heavy-based pan with all the vegetables, herbs and peppercorns. Pour in the water and set over a high heat. Bring to the boil and skim off any scum that rises to the surface.

2. Cover the pan, reduce the heat and simmer very gently for at least 1 hour. Remove from the heat and set aside to cool a little. Season to taste with salt.

3. Skim off any froth or fat on the surface, then strain through a large fine-mesh sieve into a bowl, discarding the bones, vegetables and herbs. When the broth is cold, cover and chill in the fridge overnight. Skim off any fat on the surface before using.

4. Reheat 300ml/½ pint of the chicken bone broth in a saucepan over a low to medium heat. Stir in the nori or wakame and cook for 5 minutes. Add the miso paste and stir well until dissolved. Stir in the spring onions, garlic, asparagus and tofu and simmer gently over a low to medium heat for 5 minutes.

5. Pour into 2 mugs, bowls or Chilly's Coffee Cups or Food Pots. Sprinkle with chilli and coriander (if using) and enjoy.

NOTE: ***This makes 1.2 litres/2 pints chicken bone broth. Keep the leftover broth in a sealed container in the fridge or freeze in small portions. Use it for hot drinks or to make gazpacho, soups, stews, casseroles and risotto.***

OR TRY THIS …

- Add a sliced fennel bulb and a star anise when making the broth.
- Poach an egg in some simmering broth and stir in a handful of watercress or baby spinach.
- Reheat some broth and flavour with grated fresh ginger and turmeric root, chopped lemongrass, Thai mint, coriander and chilli, plus a squeeze of lime.

D

E

F

S

We would like to thank you for purchasing this book and supporting our mission of accelerating the adoption and everyday use of reusable products.

We're excited to continue on our journey of building a future where reusables are the norm.

This would not be possible without the continued efforts from you and everyone involved in the Chilly's team.

James and Tim

Ebury Press, an imprint of Ebury Publishing
20 Vauxhall Bridge Road
London SW1V 2SA

Ebury Press is part of the Penguin Random House group of companies whose addresses can be found at global.penguinrandomhouse.com

Penguin Random House UK

Photography: Haarala Hamilton
Food Stylists: Libby Silbermann and Liberty Mendez
Design: maru studio
Production: Catherine Ngwong
Publishing Director: Elizabeth Bond
Publishing Assistant: Izzy Frost

First published by Ebury Press in 2023

www.penguin.co.uk
www.chillys.com

A CIP catalogue record for this book is available from the British Library

ISBN 978-1-52919-737-2

Printed and bound: TBB, a.s. Slovakia

The authorised representative in the EEA is Penguin Random House Ireland, Morrison Chambers, 32 Nassau Street, Dublin D02 YH68.

MIX
Paper | Supporting responsible forestry
FSC www.fsc.org FSC® C018179

Penguin Random House is committed to a sustainable future for our business, our readers and our planet. This book is made from Forest Stewardship Council® certified paper.

1

BONSAI

BON